VIOLIN TEACHING IN CLASS

A Handbook for Teachers

VIOLIN TEACHING
IN CLASS

A Handbook for Teachers

GERTRUDE COLLINS

With a Foreword by
BERNARD SHORE

Illustrations by Peter Moore

LONDON
OXFORD UNIVERSITY PRESS
NEW YORK   TORONTO
1962

Oxford University Press, Amen House, London E.C.4

GLASGOW NEW YORK TORONTO MELBOURNE WELLINGTON
BOMBAY CALCUTTA MADRAS KARACHI LAHORE DACCA
CAPE TOWN SALISBURY NAIROBI IBADAN ACCRA
KUALA LUMPUR HONG KONG

*The illustration on the front cover is taken from a photograph
by Roger Smithwright*

PRINTED IN GREAT BRITAIN

FOREWORD

Gertrude Collins is a fine violinist and a brilliant teacher, who is unsurpassed in a field she has made her own—teaching the violin in class. In this book she has generously set forth the secrets of her unique technique for the benefit and guidance of all who are engaged upon this difficult work.

The written word cannot bring to life the greatest asset of any teacher, warmth and charm of personality, but all those who have worked with Gertrude Collins will be able to read between the lines, and find particular enjoyment in this valuable book.

BERNARD SHORE

CONTENTS

INTRODUCTION

The suggestion that the violin might be taught in class was first made to me by the representative of a firm selling instruments to schools. The idea filled me with dismay, and I had no intention at that time of trying to carry out his proposal.

Soon afterwards, however, he introduced me to the Headmistress of a Primary School near my home who was extremely anxious for her pupils to learn to play an instrument, if only for a short time and whether or no they intended to make music a career.

She persuaded me to meet some of the children who were longing to play the violin with a view to teaching them in very small groups of two or three. Confronted with fourteen wide-eyed eight-year-olds clutching half-size fiddles, and finding that they could name the strings and read music a little, I capitulated and promised to form a class.

With small experience of individual teaching and none whatever of class teaching, I started off gaily with all fourteen children together.

The experiment had begun.

It was these children who proved to me that the violin could be learned in class. Eight were unusually talented, though I did not realize this at the time. One year later the class was divided into two groups of eight and six; seven are now professional players or teachers. In four years numbers had increased to about 150, mainly owing to the talent of the children and to the enthusiasm and co-operation of parents and school staff.

Not only children but parents, grandparents, the head-mistress, members of staff, and the school caretaker were all having lessons in classes; most of them were starting from the beginning, and in some homes regular practices were held for groups of children and grown-ups. The majority of the players lived within a mile of the school.

Such conditions are not normal; indeed they are very rare. Had I encountered some of the slower groups I have met since those early days I might have given up trying to teach in class, but this happy first experience encouraged me to continue the work and to experiment with ways of teaching children less musically gifted.

We now needed violas and cellos for our 'orchestra', and a viola class was started for parents and staff. At that time I had not realized that a small violin, re-strung, could be used as a substitute for a viola, and thus made available for children of Primary School age. As the school could not find a cellist willing to teach a class, one of the parents decided to have private lessons and pass on her knowledge to others. There is danger in such a procedure, but in this case it worked well because the teacher-parent was an excellent musician. Our string orchestra was almost complete and one 'family' quartet was formed.

The work was haphazard, as I knew no one else who taught in class and whom I might have consulted. Although I tried to plan the work and get help from existing national examination syllabuses, these schemes did not meet the requirements of my classes.

After experimenting for about six years I came in touch

with the Rural Music Schools Association, and this gave me the opportunity of meeting others experienced in class teaching. They suggested that I should attend their Summer School for String Teachers—an innovation in those days— and talk about my own classes.

This made me realize I had no special plan or scheme of work. It was the impetus given me by the Association which led me to analyse my way of teaching and impart my findings to others.

Since those days the plans and schemes have undergone many changes and I hope will continue to do so, but the suggestions in this book are the result of twenty years of class teaching: the outcome of an experiment with fourteen talented small children.

Before beginning instrumental work in class I had a little experience of teaching general music in a school, but my interest was in the violin. During most of my teaching life, therefore, I have been a visiting teacher in many types of schools and colleges. The work can be lonely. It is difficult to 'strike root' and feel you really belong to a school in which you give one short weekly lesson, and it is not easy to get to know your pupils. The work is often slow and frustrating, but the results can be most rewarding.

Tradition has it that instruments should be taught individually, but class teaching is now accepted by musicians and those who plan general education.

With either method, the two most important qualifications in the teacher are personality and an understanding of the basic principles of string-playing. There is no essential difference in approach. A child, whether taught privately or in class, learns to play an instrument and develop musicianship, and in both cases the training should include taking part in ensemble and orchestral work; but the problems of teaching in class are not identical with those of teaching individual pupils. For one thing there is the question of discipline. Next, every child differs musically, and in ability to manipulate an instrument. In class, good intonation may take longer to achieve, for it is difficult to learn to listen carefully when playing with others.

The first introduction to an orchestral instrument is usually made through the violin, because manipulative skill in an unnatural posture needs developing as early as possible, simultaneously with other skills.

Every instrumentalist hopes to have experience of orchestral playing, and in the average symphony orchestra violinists are needed in greater numbers than players of other instruments. If the violin is found unsuitable for any particular child there is time to change to another instrument and make good progress.

Last, but not least, a violin (together with bow and case) is still the cheapest orchestral instrument to buy.

In this book I shall deal with the class-teaching of the violin only. I have once or twice attempted to teach the viola, having been told, on good authority, that in the earliest stages the same basic principles of playing apply to both violin and viola. I have never tried to teach the cello or double bass, for I have usually been lucky enough to find specialist teachers to take pupils who wish to learn these instruments. There are circumstances, however, in which it becomes necessary to teach a second instrument, particularly in rural areas where a pupil is anxious to learn something other than the violin, or where there is no other way of building an orchestra. If this happens, the teacher should try to take lessons in cello or double-bass playing.

I

THE SET-UP

If you are qualified and prepared to teach the violin in class you may find yourself (a) in charge of all music in a school, the violin class being part of your general work, or (b) employed by an Education Authority as a specialist string teacher visiting schools, colleges, Youth Clubs, and Evening Institutes, or (c) a free-lance specialist string teacher visiting independent schools, music schools or classes arranged by an organization such as the Rural Music Schools Association.

In both (b) and (c) you will teach people of all kinds and ages, and a very quick adjustment has to be made from one type of class to another. Some teachers are best with young people; others with older children or adults.

If you are a visiting teacher a car is almost a necessity. Instruments, sometimes in large numbers, have to be carried, as well as music and tools for repairs; and teaching can suffer if it is done with an eye on the clock for fear of missing the only bus which will get you to your next class in time.

Whichever form your teaching may take it is as well to consider the following queries before starting. Some apply to school classes only but others to players of all ages.

My personal views and comments are given under each question.

1. Should lessons be compulsory or voluntary?

> Voluntary. Sometimes it may be wise to give one or two 'try-out' lessons to a whole class and then ask for volunteers.

2. Should lessons be in or out of school hours?

> This depends largely on the degree of interest shown by the head of the school and by the teacher in charge of music; also on the district in which the work is done. All violin teachers are glad to be allowed to teach during school hours, but then they must accept the fact that children will usually be graded according to their ability in general school subjects, and not as violinists. After the first year I prefer to teach violin classes out of school hours, for then children may be grouped according to their musical or manipulative ability irrespective of age or school class.

3. Should pupils pay a fee or should the lessons be free?

> Pupils should pay for their lessons, if only a small sum, towards the cost of the teacher's fees.

4. Should pupils buy their instruments and music?

> Yes. Some schools provide violins, some lend them for a limited period. But both children and parents value the instruments more if they buy them. It is a sad fact that instruments are far better cared for when owned by the pupils. Also, if the instruments are part of ordinary school equipment pupils are apt to give up on leaving school. Owning their instrument encourages them to carry on into adult life.

5. Should a child have an ear test, or a test for manipulative ability, before being allowed to join a class?

I take all who wish to learn. Where numbers have to be limited, simple manipulative tests and ear tests can be made, always remembering that if a child cannot sing in tune it does not necessarily mean that he or she is tone deaf.

6. Should pupils have had some musical training before-hand; say a little knowledge of theory and notation?

This is useful but not essential. Much is manipulative in the early stages and notation can be learned during the lessons.

7. What is the best age to start?

As early as possible. Age seven or eight, or earlier if there is a little independence of finger movement and if help can be given with practice.
For those who are looking for a worth-while amuse-ment or hobby it is never too late to begin.

8. How many pupils should there be in a class?

As few as possible. Six to eight is ideal, and never more than ten, unless for a very short period, or unless the class is taken by a very experienced teacher.

9. How long should a lesson last, and how many should there be in a week?
Forty to forty-five minutes is usual. Half an hour is too short and an hour is too long for most classes.
A lesson every day would be ideal. Usually there is one a week, but where there are two a week progress is much more noticeable.

10. Should practising be introduced at the start, or later, when pupils have a little understanding of handling the instrument?

I suggest *no* practising for the first half term or term, even if there is only one lesson a week. Make it clear however that after that period regular practice will be expected.

11. Should a left-handed person play the instrument 'the other way round'?

No. The whole instrument would have to be rebuilt. Try to persuade such people that they are lucky, as they will be able to do some things much more easily than a right-handed player.

There are occasional exceptions to this, e.g. loss of a left-hand finger or a joint which will not bend. A number of people have played left-handedly, but on the whole it is easier for future work to play the instrument in the usual way.

12. Should double-jointed people play the violin?

Yes, if they are keen to try, but the problems and difficulties are great. All one can do is to commiserate, encourage, and persevere in trying to strengthen the hands of the pupil.

It seems obvious that co-operation between school, staff and parents is necessary if the work is to succeed, and yet classes are often started without any clear understanding of how this may be achieved.

No experienced violin teacher would expect a class to play hymns (often in four flats) for School Assembly after only a couple of terms' tuition, but Heads of schools, keen to establish a school orchestra, have been known to demand this. They themselves may be fine musicians, but unless they have a clear idea of the technical difficulties of violin playing they may ask too much too soon, and bad results will discourage both teachers and players.

Fortunate is the visiting teacher who has the backing and help of one or more members of the regular staff, able and willing to be present at some of the lessons and play the piano, and possibly arrange and supervise practising between lessons. This is of infinite importance.

On the other side it is essential for the visiting teacher to be aware of the wider aspects of music in the school; to know what is being attempted, and what sort of music-language is being used—e.g., solfa or French time-names— and adjust the violin work accordingly.

It is well to spend some time in the Staff Room and if possible get to know members of the permanent staff. The teacher of needlework may be kind enough to get her pupils to make shoulder-pads for violin players, and woodwork masters may supply cases or racks for instruments, but above and beyond all this is the necessity to make social contact with others working in the school.

Even if the school owns and lends instruments, parents do not always understand that they will be responsible for upkeep and repairs, or that they will be required to buy a small amount of music; nor do they realize how much they may do at home to help the children. There is an intermediate stage in learning the violin: the period when the initial thrill of carrying a violin case has waned, and the first easy and amusing lessons are followed by harder ones which must be practised in order to acquire the technique necessary for playing really interesting and more beautiful music. This is the time when parents can give invaluable encouragement. Some have confessed to a certain amount of coercion, and others have resorted to bribery. ('I make no promises, but if you can play these exercises really well at the end of term your father and I might help you to buy that cricket bat.')

A letter to parents from the Head of the school or, better still, an invitation to a meeting at which matters can be explained and questions answered, are good ways of making a start. Not all homes are fortunate enough to have a piano or a quiet room for practising. The best help comes from parents or relations who are themselves musicians; but it is equally true that a parent who plays the violin can be a menace.

Many schools are profoundly influenced by local conditions, and until their particular problems are solved it is no use drawing up elaborate schemes of work. In some country districts special buses collect children after school and take them to their homes. Unless times of departure can be adjusted, lessons or practice cannot be held immediately after the close of school. Again, the only room available for violin lessons may be unsuitable for various reasons. As work grows it is difficult to fit in new classes. The visiting teacher should try to save long journeys by arranging lessons on one particular day at schools in the same area.

2

INTRODUCING INSTRUMENTAL
WORK TO A SCHOOL

There are many opportunities for young people to hear
instruments and to see them played, but I have known
children volunteer for instrumental classes through a mis-
understanding or parental wishful thinking. There was the
child who joined a cello class and only found courage at the
end of the year to tell the teacher that she had really been
expecting to have bass recorder lessons all the time. A
reluctant small boy, brought to the first violin lesson by
Mother, was questioned by the teacher, who found that he
had never heard or seen a violin. Mother supplied the reasons
for his arrival. 'Well you see, we put him to the Church choir,
but he didn't seem to get on with it, so we put him to the
piano, but he didn't get on with that either—couldn't
manage two lines at once—so when we heard that violin
classes were starting, we thought we'd put him to the
violin.'

Some kind of introduction is necessary and the three most
usual ways of introducing the violin are as follows:

1. If violin classes are to be started from scratch, it may be a
   good plan for the teacher to play the instrument to the
   children and explain how it works.
2. Children from another school who play already can be
   asked to demonstrate.

3. Perhaps the most successful way of introducing children to the instrument is to give a first lesson to a group with others watching and listening. It is even better, if there is time, to allow every child to hold the violin and bow and pluck an open-string piece.

After an introduction to instrumental music, it is often wise for a visiting teacher at a new school to let a few weeks elapse before starting actual lessons. The time can be spent in overhauling instruments, getting to know the children and taking measurements in order to find violins of suitable size for each child. Office work has to be organized; money problems settled; letters written to parents, and, if the teacher of music is willing, attendance of the violin teacher arranged at one or two music lessons. When everything is in order and planned as far as possible it will be found that time has not been wasted, even if actual violin lessons begin half a term late.

Conditions for Teaching

All teachers of music dream of a music-room, quiet, warm and well-lit, with space to move, a good piano at correct pitch, storage space for music, racks for instruments, music-stands in good condition, a blackboard and solid wooden kitchen chairs. If there are any desks they should be easily movable. (A radiogram, record library and a tape-recorder are pleasant to find, but not essential.)

We are far more likely to find ourselves giving lessons in a noisy room, perhaps with roller-skating in the playground outside, or trying to teach without making a noise so as not to disturb other lessons. In some schools it is impossible to teach in the same room every week. A class may be transferred to the canteen where meals are being prepared or cleared up, or to a corner of the assembly hall, or the staff room. Perhaps a cloakroom is the most disconcerting, with its constant traffic of people coming and going on their lawful occasions.

Sometimes the room is cold and dark, with desks and benches that are impossible to move.

We often teach without the help of a piano, and this is of no great importance, but where there *is* a piano it is often a semitone flat, and this makes transposition necessary.

Instruments are damaged when no storage room is available and they have to be left in a cloakroom. Music stands are always losing rivets, and if there are separate chairs they are usually of the stacking variety, which makes good playing posture impossible. These conditions cannot always be helped. The school authorities are as worried about them as the teachers.

If there is any choice, try above all to obtain:

1. A quiet room free from interruptions.
2. Permission to use the same room for each lesson.
2. A warm, light room, in which there is space to move freely.
4. A blackboard, or some other device for displaying charts.
5. A room with a piano and wooden chairs.

This list is given in the order of importance. Do not, for instance, choose a small dark room merely because it contains a piano.

Sometimes in an emergency it is necessary to take a class in a passage or storeroom, where there is no room to play. This may offer an opportunity to show pupils how to clean and overhaul their instruments instead of trying to play in impossible conditions.

Equipment

It is the responsibility of the teacher to see that instruments are in good order, and maintained in good working order.

It saves time if the teacher can do much of this work himself, but whether or not this is possible the work must be done. A violin in good condition is difficult enough to tune and play, but one with ill-fitting pegs, and a badly-set bridge, to mention only two defects, is quite impossible to play, and if the hair of the bow is worn and greasy matters are even worse.

It is far more important to have a well-fitted instrument than a good one. Pegs must fit properly; the nut at the peg-box end of the fingerboard must be the right height, and strings evenly spaced. The fingerboard must be glued properly to the neck. (Children have been seen trying to play with a loose fingerboard slipping about under the strings.) The strings must be the right height above the fingerboard; the bridge must have its feet properly set, be the right height, and have the right curve, and strings evenly placed. The tailpiece gut must be the right length, so that the tailpiece is in the right place.

The bow must not be warped (a crooked bow can be re-sprung); it must have a reasonable amount of hair, and a screw that has not rusted into the eyelet.

All these defects can be seen from the outside, even by inexperienced teachers, but it needs more expert knowledge to know whether the neck is set correctly; whether certain cracks can be mended easily or whether the instrument is badly damaged. Some teachers are specialists who can deal with these matters and also set soundposts successfully, but as a rule repairs are best left to a craftsman of experience.

The soundpost is wedged between back and belly of the violin, just behind the foot of the bridge on the E string side, and there must be one! I have found soundposts glued in, and on two occasions soundposts were held up by a nail driven through the back of the instrument. How these 'repairs' were accomplished is beyond comprehension!

Every violin should be fitted with a chin-rest. They are of

many shapes and sizes, but a large one, even on a small fiddle, is usually the most satisfactory. The small bar, or kidney-shaped chin-rest, makes it difficult for most pupils to balance the instrument properly between jaw and shoulder. A good chin-rest should be on the violin when the pupil first handles it. It is part of the outfit, and an important part. A pupil of mine, having been told at the first lesson that he must buy a chin-rest, returned the following week with this message: 'My Dad says I can have a chin-rest when I can play the violin.'

I insist on a pad or shoulder rest. Some violinists do not use them, but for the average pupil one or the other is necessary for comfort and correct posture. The comfort of a balanced hold is of the utmost importance, and this is generally achieved by having a chin-rest and pad. Every member of the class may need a different amount of padding. I use pounds of cotton wool during the first term trying to get the right size, shape and thickness for each pupil. In the case of growing children adjustments are necessary from time to time. A rubber band to hold the pad in place on the instrument is invaluable. The patent shoulder rest can be helpful, but is not suitable for everyone and it is often too expensive for the average class pupil.

Size of Instruments

Instruments are made in many sizes, officially full, three-quarters, half, quarter, and eighth, but the last two rarely concern the class teacher. The sizes are not exact. For instance, it is possible to have a large threequarter or a small half. If the right size cannot be obtained it is better to have a violin too small rather than too large. Children up to the age of ten or eleven probably need a half or threequarter size instrument. Those of eleven years and older will need three-quarter or full-size violins, but there is no hard and fast rule.

Most adults need full-size instruments. A quick way of measuring is to put the violin in the playing position and ask the pupil to put the palm of the left hand round the end of the scroll, and the fingers round towards the pegbox. If they can reach this the violin is likely to be the right size. The arm in playing position should not touch the body of the violin.

When handing over instruments to pupils for the first time, see they are clean and polished, free from fingermarks and powdered rosin. This will encourage the players to take a pride in the appearance of their instruments, and keep them clean—a useful habit, even if the instruments are not very good ones.

Rosin and a cloth for cleaning should be in every violin case.

The Arrangement of the Class-Room

It is a curious fact that the way in which a class-room is arranged at the first lesson tends to become a habit and difficult to alter at a later stage. So before lessons begin, make a point of visiting the room in which you are to teach and studying its lay-out. Decide where the pupils will stand or sit; where you will hang charts, and which is the best place for the piano if one is available.

It is a great advantage to have a focal point to which all players will look when practising posture drills, bowing movements, etc. The focal point can be a blackboard, a window, a picture, a vase of flowers—indeed almost anything. I use a set of charts. They are slung over a blackboard on an easel, but if the school is modern enough to have wall blackboards only, the charts will stand on a chair placed on a desk or on top of an upright piano. (The copying of published violin pieces on to charts or blackboard is usually an infringement of copyright, but exercises, scales, traditional tunes and one's own 'bits and pieces' can always be written up with perfect safety. Each pupil of course will have his or her individual copy of music even if it is not always used in class.)

Pupils sit and stand alternately during earlier lessons, and as violin stands are apt to be knocked over when changing from one position to another, for a term or two I use charts only. As the work advances charts are discarded and stands introduced with copies of music on them for each pupil.

Arrange seats or standing positions facing the focal point and in a block as though the players were a section of an orchestra. Teach mostly from the bowing side, as this makes it possible to see all the pupils all the time. If there is a piano and you are going to use it, set up your class in the way indicated in either of these diagrams:

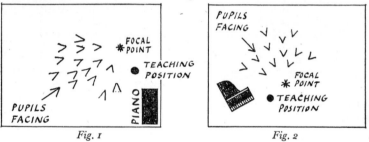

Fig. 1   Fig. 2

In both cases teach from piano, focal point, or own instrument position except when individual attention is needed. So often one meets this arrangement:

Fig. 3

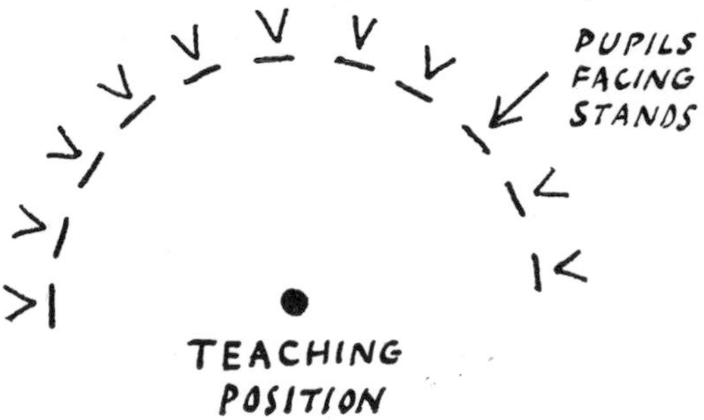

All pupils are thus at a different angle to the teaching position and if stands are used it is impossible to see the players. At best it is only possible to watch one or two at a time.

The block formation is far more satisfactory, but if a classroom has desks which cannot be moved, the following arrangement is suggested:

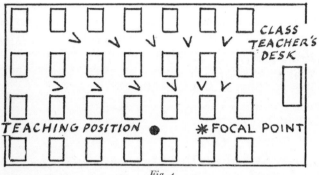

Fig. 4

Pupils are not so cramped if they stand sideways in the aisles between desks.

Repairs

Repairs, such as replacing broken strings, take up much time in class and are best dealt with before or after the lesson.

I always carry strings with me, and in case an instrument comes to grief in class, it is useful to have a spare violin (tuned) and bow in reserve.

Spare bridges, varying in size, are sometimes needed. If a bridge breaks I find one as nearly like the broken one as possible and slip it into the right place. This enables the pupil to practise for the next week. I take the bits home and cut a new bridge the exact size of the original bridge, and fit it at the start of the next lesson, taking my own bridge back again.

3

GENERAL NOTES FOR TEACHERS

Most string players, no matter what method they adopt, will agree that good posture, relaxed and confident movements, and ear training are essential basic principles of string playing. Teachers differ enormously in their ideas as to how to lay the foundations of these principles. I can only put forward opinions based on my own experiences.

1. A plan of work is essential, not only a general scheme, but a plan for each term and each lesson. The plan can be abandoned at any moment in order to follow profitable red herrings, but it helps one to cover all the necessary ground-work. There should be one aim to every lesson.

2. Keep a note of work done in class, and home-work set for the following week. It is difficult, especially for a visiting teacher who may have many classes at the same stage, to remember exactly what was done at the previous lesson, and a brief record enables one to approach the next class with authority. The notes do not take long to write.

3. Choice of the right word at the right moment comes with experience. Clear instructions and economy of words are important and newcomers to the work would do well to consider exactly what they want to say at the next lesson.

4. A class needs to be disciplined, so that all players do the same thing at the same moment. Work will be eased later on if this is clearly understood in the first one or two lessons. Unbearable noises will break out when tension is released if the lesson has been unplanned and the minds of the pupils are muddled.

I work my beginners very hard for the first term, keeping them going with one thing after another, so that there is constant change, and no time to do anything but what I ask them to do. If they cannot 'take it' at the start, you may be sure they are unlikely to make the grade.

After the first term, when the class is used to this procedure, it is quite easy to plan for moments of relaxation between periods of concentration.

5. Try to teach one thing at a time. This is not always possible with an instrument such as the violin. Ears, eyes, manipulative movements which are different for both arms and hands, and an 'unnatural' posture, all have to be co-ordinated in the end; but try to train one sense first, then travel to another, then combine them. For instance, when dealing with intonation, it is necessary for a beginner to concentrate on listening and the muscular control of the left hand : do not ask the players to read from music and keep a straight bow as well. Keep left and right hands separate as long as you can without the class losing interest and feeling frustrated. Almost invariably when watching other teachers in class and noting that progress is particularly good, I find they have kept the manipulation of the two hands separate far longer than I myself would dare.

It is easy to forget what it feels like to be a beginner and one is apt to expect too much from pupils starting to play the instrument. I suggest it may be salutary for the teacher to try playing the violin the wrong way round. (Violin in right hand, bow in left.) There is no need to rebuild and restring the instrument. The exercise will bring back recollections of the difficulties encountered in early days of playing.

6. The violin lesson should, if possible, be a music lesson, but this is difficult to achieve. In order to produce music from a violin, a considerable amount of manipulative skill has to be acquired; the balance of the violin hold; the bow hold; the drawing of the bow across the strings; the placing of the fingers of the left hand, etc.

Much of this will have to be learned through drills in class, but exercises and drills can be rhythmical, if not always tuneful, and children can become interested in musical sounds, apart from tune playing.

7. Ear training should be part of every lesson. Drills and exercises, so necessary for acquiring technique, are often carried out in a mechanical manner with the ears practically asleep, but ear-training can be introduced into this part of the lesson by varying the rhythm and pitch of each exercise, and the quality of the sound—even when playing pizzicato.

When taking some classes it seems almost impossible to consider these things, so taken up is one by the difficulties of physical movements, but at least one can try!

8. Theory and notation can quite easily be introduced throughout the violin lessons, particularly if at first pupils do not see the signs until *after* they have heard the sounds.

I have lately taught more by demonstration and have given every encouragement to pupils to play by ear and produce the sounds *first*, but I take good care that the notation of those sounds is up in front of them. Then a lesson or so later we reverse the process, reading to produce the sound.

9. Try to plan a lesson so that the following points are covered:

   (a) Revision of something done before, disguised in as many ways as possible.

   (b) Some new technical or manipulative work, e.g. new fingering pattern or new kind of bowing.

   (c) Some piece or passage incorporating (b).

   (d) A moment of particularly careful listening.

   (e) Notation, reading, or theory.

   (f) Make an attempt to play something well within the power of the class really musically. This can be done even with pizzicato open string pieces in the first or second lessons if phrasing is considered.

   (g) When telling a class what is to be practised, show *how* it is to be done.

   (h) Try to time the lesson so that the pupils can play something well by the end of it, and leave with a sense of achievement.

10. Class work is not an end in itself, and should be limited to one, two or three years, according to circumstances. It has its place in any general scheme of instrumental work, and the most satisfactory result any teacher can experience is to find that all the pupils in a class wish to have individual lessons.

   It is well to bear this in mind, as an endless vista of class work can be depressing, but at least a large number of people have had the opportunity of learning to play an instrument.

11. The violin is not everybody's instrument. It is the able pupil, or the one who works hard, who is likely to go on playing in adult life. Do not therefore give all your care and attention to very slow pupils, or those who will not

practise. They are unlikely to make the grade, and should be allowed to drop out after a reasonable period. Occasionally, but very rarely, one meets a child of exceptional talent. Advise individual lessons at once, even for no fee, for such work is always worth while.

12. Try not to get bogged down with learning notes, especially at first. Concentrate on *how* to play the instrument and keep exercises and pieces short, so that there is a minimum of note-learning.

13. Always try to be in the class-room before the pupils arrive. The procedure of the teacher entering after the class has assembled does not seem to work with instrumental teaching.

14. Use any props necessary, e.g. marks on fingerboards to help hand formation, but do without if possible and always get rid of them as soon as they have served their purpose.

15. The piano is not essential for violin class work, but it can be helpful as long as it is not used too much and too loudly. People, particularly children, learn by imitation. It is far more important to teach with the violin in hand, but in the early stages a piano can make the work more interesting, and if well played can indicate phrasing, mood, and quality of tone, and keep a class playing together without the necessity of shouting 1, 2, 3, 4, or stamping a foot. I do not find it of much help in intonation.

The piano should usually be played quietly to encourage listening, and only with the simple, harmonic progressions to help with bowing rhythms, or pieces.

Sometimes a keen music teacher on the staff of the school will offer to attend the violin class and play the piano. This can be of the greatest help, but if the pianist is extremely facile on the keyboard the sounds can be

3

so exciting and the harmonic progressions so complicated that young pupils cannot hear what they are supposed to be doing. Simple diatonic progressions are advised as a background.

16. In the early stages of class work it is fairly easy to co-ordinate exercises, scales, and pieces in one lesson, or over a short period of two or three lessons. As work progresses things become more complicated and it may be necessary to introduce a technical exercise several weeks before beginning a new piece.

In still more advanced work, such as position work or shifts, it may be necessary to do technical exercises for their own sake, but on the whole it is better to apply the technical exercise to the music in hand as soon as possible.

Practising

No hard and fast rules can be laid down, because so much depends on the type of school in which one is teaching, its geographical situation, and the attitude of the regular staff.

Assuming that one lesson a week is given, I now use this plan:

First Term. No practising for the first four or five lessons, then a quarter of an hour five times between lessons.

Second and Third Terms. Twenty minutes five times between lessons, or more.

In the second year, half an hour each day, or more.

This is the minimum time if practising is done at home and parents are usually notified of the arrangement. Home-work cards are used in some cases, and there are schools which award marks or colours for practising. It depends on the general procedure at the school.

The school in which a member of staff supervises practice nearly always produces the best results.

In any case the pupil must be shown *how* to practise and how to divide up the time allotted. This is not easy to teach, but an effort must be made, for as students most of us have wasted untold time by useless repetitive practising. It takes experience and much thought to waste no time, but perhaps the teacher can help a little.

If one expects much from a pupil one may sometimes get it; expect nothing and you will usually get nothing. I have tried both ways!

Excuses for having done no practice are of infinite number and variety. 'I live in a flat'; 'I had to do school homework'; 'Father can't stand the noise'; 'Please Miss, I've had twins and Mother says I mustn't wake them'; 'We had visitors'; 'I had to get my hair cut.' That is why the teacher should get in contact with parents whenever possible and explain how much they can help the children by encouraging practice. Many enjoy their lessons and want to play the violin, but cannot discipline themselves to practise at home where there are sure to be distractions. In the case of a string instrument the major problem of tuning arises. Even if pupils can hear whether an instrument is in tune they have not always the strength to turn the pegs, and adult help is needed.

All one can do in the early stages is to create the right conditions for practising. Make clear some definite plan. Tell pupils how often and how long they should practise, how and what to practise, and emphasize that all repetitive work should be done with thought.

Even when one tries to do all this children will still come for lessons having done little or no work in between. Bullying, cajolery, even bribery may have to be resorted to, though in some cases hearing a great artist play, or working for an examination or concert, may act as an incentive.

Practically every book written on playing the violin contains a chapter on practising. I quote at random, 'Think quickly, play slowly'. 'The brain must be in command, the fingers obey'. 'Never play straight through a piece regardless of mistakes; always stop and correct'. 'The ear must be alert'. All admirable advice, but you and I have to get it to register in the mind of nine-year-old John, who is equally interested in railways and frog-spawn, or fourteen-year-old Mavis, keen on swimming and beginning to take a pride in long, well-cared-for varnished nails. There have been a few occasions on which I had to provide scissors and a large piece of paper and get practically every child in the class to cut his or her nails. Sometimes it has been a losing battle, and long painted nails have triumphed over the wish to play the violin.

It is not easy to make pupils want to practise, and this is where the teacher's own attempts at practising and playing become so important. What is needed is a practising apprenticeship. I shall never forget the first time I heard my own teacher rehearse with a pianist for a Sonata recital, and later on, from another room, heard him practising his own part as a result of that rehearsal; or the first time I heard a professional quartet rehearse.

One wishes all young players could overhear some good practising. It is something they seldom experience. It is talked about and written about, but that is not enough.

4

AN OUTLINE OF A SCHEME
OF CLASS WORK

There are nine stages for the purpose of this book. After
Stage I all stages are based on 'finger patterns' (most violin
teachers understand the meaning of this term) which have a
close link with key and interval.

$$o \quad = \text{open strings}$$
$$\text{numbers} \quad = \text{fingers}$$
$$\_ \quad = \text{a whole tone}$$
$$\wedge \quad = \text{a semitone}$$

There are four main finger patterns:

1. $o - 1 - \overset{\frown}{23} - 4$ Pattern I
2. $o - \overset{\frown}{12} - 3 - 4$,,   II
3. $o - 1 - 2 - \overset{\frown}{34}$,,   III
4. $\overset{\frown}{o1} - 2 - 3 - 4$,,   IV

These are used in many combinations across the strings
and do not always begin a tone or semitone from the open
strings, but they are the basic finger patterns.

Some exceptions occur with chromatic moves and aug-
mented intervals in minor scales.

FIRST SCHEME

Stage I

A. General handling of the instrument.
B. Pizzicato open strings.

C. Notation of the open string sounds.
D. Tuning.
E. Violin hold.
F. Bow hold.

Stage II

A. Placing bow on strings.
B. Bow elevations across strings.
C. Rhythmical movement of bow.
D. Building up of left hand fingering:
   $0 - 1 - \widehat{23} - 4$ (Pattern I):
   Left hand building can be introduced either with violin
   in under-arm position (like a guitar) or shoulder position.
E. Exercises and tunes (pizzicato on one string).

Stage III

A. Gradual joining together of left hand and bow.
B. Introduction of open string scales.
   G.D.A. 1 octave up and down.
C. Rhythmic bowings to well-known tunes.
   Different speeds of bow movement, different parts of the
   bow.
D. Slurs.
E. Tune playing. Folk tones, hymns and carols.
   Fingering all $0 - 1 - \widehat{23} - 4$.
   See Comments on Stages I, II, and III.

Stage IV

A. Finger pattern $0 - \widehat{12} - 3 - 4$ (Pattern II) (or scales
   starting on 3rd finger: C and G).
B. Bowing. Consolidation of Stage III.

Stage V

Mixture of Patterns I and II

$0 - 1 - \widehat{23} - 4$ ⎱ The 2nd finger moves its position
$0 - \widehat{12} - 3 - 4$ ⎰ across the strings.

A. Keys. Major. G two octaves

It is also possible to play in the key of

D (no C♯ on G string)
C (no F♮ on E string)
F (on G and D strings only)

Minor. G.D.A. open string melodic form upwards only.

B. Bowings. Uneven speeds of bow movement, legato and broken slurs, uneven slurs, staccato, martelé, slow spiccato, and smooth bow changing.

Stage VI

Sharp Scales

A. 1. Finger pattern $0 - 1 - 2 - \widehat{34}$ (Pattern III) or 1st-finger scales. B.E.A. one octave
   2.   A   two octaves (III and I)
                  D   extended across all four strings (I, II, and III)
   3. 1st-finger melodic minor scales (I, II, III)

B. Bowings. Consolidation of Stage V.
   See Comments on Stages IV, V and VI including theory and notation, vibrato, etc.

Stage VII

Flat Scales

A. 1. Finger pattern $\widehat{01} - 2 - \widehat{34}$ (Pattern III flat).
      1st-finger scales. B♭ E♭ A♭ one octave
   2.   B♭   two octaves
                         A♭   two octaves
   3. Extended scales. F on D to B♭ on E, but not lower on D and G strings.

4. Scales in sixths.

B. Bowings. Continuation of Stage VI.

Stage VIII

A. 1. Backward and forward movement of 1st finger. A mixture of patterns III flat, II, and use of finger pattern IV:

(a) ô1 – 2 – ŝ4   (Pattern III)
(b) o – 1̂2 – 3 – (4) (Pattern II)
(c) ô1 – 2 – 3 – 4 (Pattern IV)

This movement is necessary for keys C and F.

2. Minor scales and arpeggios. Both forms.
3. Chromatic scales.
4. Scales in sixths.

B. Bowing development as in VI and VII.
C. Theory and notation.
D. Some other incentives.

Stage IX

A. Position Work. Playing in different positions without shifts.
B. Reading in positions.
C. Shifts from one position to another.

It is impossible to estimate how long a class will take to work through all these stages. Some classes perish in the earlier ones. This frequently happens when a class is made up of individuals of differing ability. Re-grouping takes place, and some pupils give up. Perhaps it is safe to say that stages I to VI take two to three years according to age and ability; stages VII to IX two to three years.

Most teachers use the same order of finger patterns from Stage I to Stage V. In the later stages the order is varied according to circumstances.

Follows First Scheme from Stage I to Stage VI.
Stage VII. Position Work in Pattern III.
Stage VIII. Flats in Pattern III.
Stage IX. As VIII in First Scheme.

THIRD SCHEME

Follows First Scheme from Stage I to Stage V.

Stage VI

1. ⌢01 – 2 – 3 – 4 (Pattern IV is introduced on E as in
   key C, while 0 – ⌢12 – 3 – 4 (Pattern II) is still used on
   A and D strings.
2. ⌢01 – 2 – 3 – 4 (Pattern IV on A string as in key F,
   while 0 – ⌢12 – 3 – 4 (Pattern II) is still used on D and
   G strings.

Stage VII

1. 0 – 1 – 2 – ⌢34 (Pattern III)
   1st-finger scales. B.E.A. one octave, sharps.
2. A. two octaves.

Stage VIII

1. ⌢01 – 2 – ⌢34 (Pattern III flat).
   1st-finger scales B♭ E♭ A♭, one octave, flats.
2. Chromatic scales.
3. Minor scales.

Stage IX

Position work as in First Scheme.

Note

It must be remembered that viola, cello, and bass have as their natural keys C, G, and often F. Keys D and A sometimes present technical problems for these instruments. If, therefore, the start of an orchestra is of first importance, the Third Scheme may be more appropriate.

5

THE PLAN IN DETAIL: STAGE I

Provided one has the technique, it is easy to show a class how to play a technical exercise. It is more difficult to express this action in words. Most difficult of all is to convey that technical exercises are but a means to musicianship, and unless this is constantly kept in mind the exercises will be of little worth.

Not all the drills suggested in the plan will be necessary in every class; in fact the fewer the drills the less waste of time, but there are always some pupils who cannot learn so quickly as others, and by changing the form of the drills, the slower pupils can be helped and the quicker ones are made to feel they are doing something new.

Drills help members of a class to do the same things at the same time, but should never be used for their own sake.

Stage I

A. General handling of the instrument.
B. Pizzicato open strings.
C. Notation of the open string sounds.
D. Tuning.
E. Violin hold.
F. The Bow.

The First Lesson in Playing

A. 1. All preliminary organization has been completed, and if possible the class-room arranged and violins tuned before the pupils come in for their first lesson.

An instrument in its case should be on the ground on the left hand side of each chair with the narrow end of the case pointing away from the teacher. If pupils bring violins with them, ask them to sit and place their cases in this position. (It is unsafe to open cases balanced on knees.)

2. Undo the cases and lift violin out by the *neck* (not the fingerboard which is apt to come unglued).

3. With the strings facing the pupil, and scroll up, rest the violin on the knees. Later this becomes known as the 'tuning position' (see facing page).

B. 4. Ask pupils to pluck the string on their right (E). Start immediately to play on the piano or violin a tune with a steady, clear, pulse, quietly and rhythmically, and the whole class will pluck E strings in time with the pulse.

5. At an appropriate moment in the tune, ask for the next string to be plucked, and continue with the third and fourth. Pupils will have heard the sound of the four open strings and will have played something right away.

6. Tuning. This has to be done, even if for many months (years in some cases) children cannot do it without aid. At the first lesson the E string is tuned with the adjuster. Turn to the left to flatten the pitch, then to the right to correct pitch; the teacher playing the E sound.

7. Learn the names of the strings, E.A.D.G.

8. Words in sound, such as EGG, DAD, DEED, GAG, EDGE, AGE, etc. These can be given by letters or by sound, or pupils can make up their own words and play them to the class.

Sound and name of string have now been linked.

9. A first attempt must now be made to hold and balance the violin between the jaw and the shoulder. For this a pad is usually essential and the teacher should have an

Fig. 5

ample supply of shoulder pads of different size and thickness in the classroom.

The next step is to introduce the written notation of those sounds:

Sounds – Name – Notation

C. 10. A short piece, written on a chart (open strings, continuous crotchets) can now be tried, the teacher playing a tune on piano or violin, the pupils playing in the tuning position. The pulse will be taken for granted. The staff is introduced immediately and the placing of the sounds G D A E shown on it. Pupils often say that they cannot read music, but if, having shown them where G is placed on the staff, you point to D and ask 'what is this' they will tell you its name without hesitation. The same will happen with A and E. They expect to see only those four signs for the sounds they have made and heard ('and you told me you couldn't read music'—pleased smiles spread over your pupils' faces). Alternatively the first phrase could be taught by ear and number: 4 Gs, 4 Ds, 4 As, 2 Es, 2 As. Play this two or three times and then show them the sounds written on the charts. ('This is what you have been playing. Here are your 4 Gs, 4 Ds, etc.—now go on to the end.')

11. Watch your pupils put their instruments away. Explain why we wrap them up for protection and the need for care in handling and carrying the instrument. Give instructions for making shoulder pads.

12. When the violin is not in use it should be placed in the case by the side of the pupil.

This is the absolute maximum of material I normally give in the first lesson. It is not always possible to go so far.

To continue to give detailed specimen lessons throughout this book is not possible. From now on, tuning drills, violin hold drills, and bow hold drills will be given under their own headings. The teacher can plan his or her lessons by picking out from each section those items which will suit a class at any particular stage.

TUNING

D. Tune one string at each of the first four lessons. Tune to a sound given by the teacher (on violin, not piano).

First Lesson. Tune string E using adjuster.
Second Lesson. Tuning position. Tune string A.

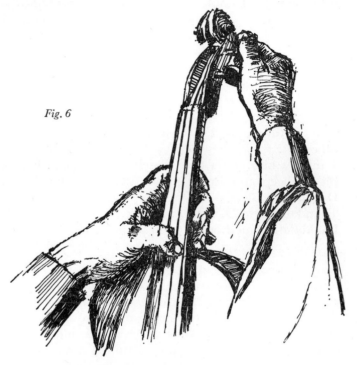

Fig. 6

(a) Find out which peg turns the A string.
(b) Place the right hand on this peg.
(c) Have the left hand at the base of the neck on the other side, with the thumb ready to pluck.
(d) Press the peg into its socket and against the other hand and turn towards you. Pluck. (Sound will be flat.)
(e) Still pressing, turn peg away from you, plucking meanwhile to hear whether you are reaching the sound given by the teacher.

Third Lesson. Tune string D.   ⎫   Same procedure
Fourth Lesson. Tune string G.   ⎭   as for A.

There may be trouble, but at least the exercises will encourage the habit of tuning before playing. Help must be given. The teacher will have to do most of the tuning.

Alternative suggestions

1. As the pupils get out their instruments, play a sound. What is it? That is the string to be tuned today.
2. A pupil arrives early. Tune the fiddle and ask him or her to act as tuner, playing the note and asking the others to tune to it.
3. Tuning a fifth. To a tune the class knows, e.g. Baa-Baa Black Sheep, usually at a pitch they can sing. D to A. Doh, Soh.
    Then later G to D. D to A. A to E.
    Use different methods at each lesson.

Note

Always honour the request of a pupil who stops playing because he thinks his instrument is out of tune. This can be infuriating when it happens at a moment when you are trying to make the class concentrate on something. The violin may be perfectly in tune when tested, but the interruption shows that the importance of tuning is recognized.

THE VIOLIN HOLD

E. There are several holds which can be of use in classwork.
I. Tuning position, i.e. violin upright on knee, strings towards player (fig. 7).
II. Under-arm or banjo position. Usually sitting, violin under right arm, strings away from body. The scroll should be on a level with the left shoulder and not too close to the body (fig. 8). Place the right hand fingers along the fingerboard on the

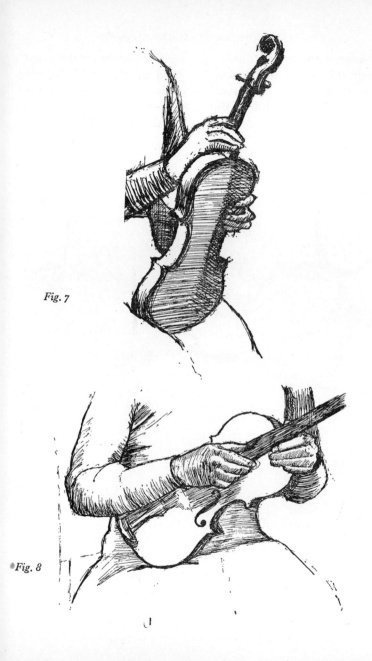

Fig. 7

Fig. 8

side nearest the ground and pluck the strings with the right thumb. The left hand can either hold up the violin lightly when open strings are plucked, or later be placed in the correct playing position of the fingers—left hand and arm in one straight line. Care must be taken that the left hand does

Fig. 9

not become cramped by allowing the scroll to be too low, or the violin to be held too close to the body. The under-arm position is used for note-learning in class. Pupils can see what their fingers are doing. If the official shoulder hold is used in the early stages, posture often becomes slack.

III. The rest position. The usual position of carrying a violin with the right arm protecting the bridge. Used when not manipulating the violin, for both standing and sitting.

Fig. 10

IV. Shoulder hold. Three basic angles for holding the violin must be considered.

(a) Strings parallel with the floor. As the strings slant from the bridge down to the pegbox, the scroll should be a little higher than the chin-rest.

(b) The violin should tilt towards the E string side but only far enough to enable the bow to rest with its natural weight on all four strings.

(c) The angle at which the violin should be held from the body varies between over-the-left-shoulder to in-front-of-the-nose. It is more comfortable for the left arm if the violin is over the shoulder, but if held *too* far over it is impossible to bow with a straight bow and a relaxed arm, therefore bring the violin to the front far enough to bow easily. It is not really possible to judge this angle exactly until the bow is used.

In theory these angles are the same for everyone, but in fact they differ according to the build of the pupil, length of arm, neck, and shape of jaw. It is of the utmost importance to make the pupil comfortable, and a pad or shoulder rest is generally essential. (Sometimes the chin-rest has to be changed.) It is possible to use a shoe-cleaning pad, but a home-made one is easier to adjust. Ask each member of the class to make a bag, approximately 6×4 inches in size, stuff it with cotton wool, and bring it to the next lesson or at the earliest possible moment. One side of the bag must be left open so that a good fit can be obtained by adding or taking out wool. The pad should be looped round the chin-rest with tape and safety pins. Elastic should not be used, but a rubber band is useful to hold the pad in place later.

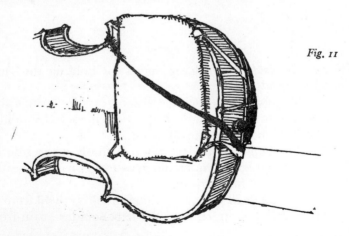

Fig. 11

There is no movement in every day life which corresponds to the position of the left arm when holding a violin. It is unnatural and can be extremely tiring (even painful) in the early stages. This is due to stiffness, and the following exercises may be helpful in obtaining relaxation of the arm, which should never be strained under the instrument. They can be practised in between attempts to hold the instrument correctly.

Relaxation exercises (without the instrument):

1. Elbows together in front of chest. Take right arm away, leaving left elbow in place, and left hand about twelve inches from face. Jerk the hand and thumb round to the left as though you were hitch-hiking and asking for a lift.
2. Hold the left elbow in the palm of the right hand, with left hand level with the face and about twelve inches away.

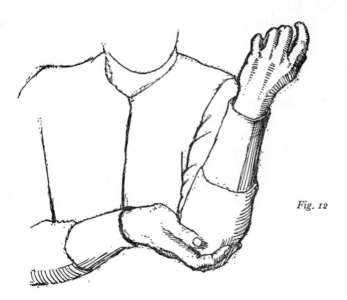

Fig. 12

Take the weight of left arm in right hand. Jog the left elbow up and down with the right hand, keeping the left hand loose. The right hand holds up the left arm so that the left arm muscles are as relaxed as possible.

3. Try to get the same 'heavy' feeling in the left hand as in Drill 2, but without holding it up with the right hand.

It is better for posture to have pupils standing for the following drills. Later they can learn to sit correctly for playing.

(a) Stand with feet apart, well-balanced and straight, in such a position that the left shoulder is slightly towards the focal point or charts, not at right angles. Do not twist the body (fig. 13).

(b) Keeping the head erect turn it to the left and look at the charts.

(c) Place the violin on your left shoulder, scroll pointing to charts.

(d) Put the left side of your jaw on the chin-rest. (Stress again and again that the violin is held and balanced between the jaw and the shoulder, and *not* held up by the left hand, which should be left free for playing.)

(e) Balance and hold the violin, fitted with chin-rest and pad, between the jaw and the shoulder, and place the left arm across the body (fig. 14). As the shoulders should not be hunched it can easily be recognized how essential the pad is for the comfort of the player, and why more stuffing is needed for longer-necked people. This is the time for making adjustments, but remember that growing children will need pads to be altered at frequent intervals.

(f) While holding the violin between jaw and shoulder move the left hand about. Touch scroll, then the bridge. Bring hand and arm under the violin and look at the palm of the hand.

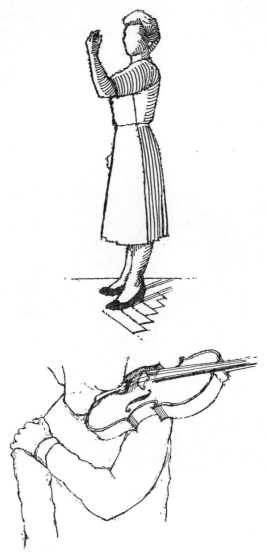

Fig. 13

Fig. 14

See that the stance is still correct, that tummies do not stick out, and that the pupil does not hold his breath. For open string pizzicato and later open string bowing, and in the early stages when trying to make pupils comfortable, it may be useful to put the left hand in the following position:

   (g) *Thumb hold*. Bring hand and arm under violin and allow the body of the violin near the neck to rest on the tip of the left thumb. Place the tips of the fingers round the ribs of the instrument. Ease the left elbow in front of the chest.

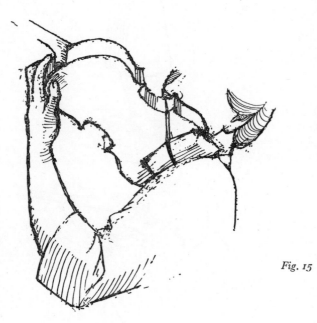

Fig. 15

V. *Final stage of shoulder hold*

From the thumb hold position the hand can be taken down the neck, the bottom joint of the 1st finger (where the finger joins the hand) touching lightly on the neck, and the tip of the thumb level with the top of the finger-board, the hand and arm being in a straight line. To overcome the collapsed left wrist (a common fault) insist that the violin is

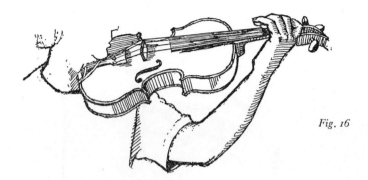

Fig. 16

not held up by the hand; that only the cushion of the thumb and the side of the finger touch the neck. Saying 'Thumbs up to the ceiling' may help, or, as I heard a teacher say 'Hitch-hike thumbs!' This remark had the effect of keeping left thumbs loose.

This final, correct shoulder hold is, as a rule, not introduced until fingering has been started in the under-arm position. The shoulder hold should be attempted and practised over and over again during the early lessons. It helps the pupil to be at ease with the instrument. Stress constantly the need for poise and comfort. There should be no vice-like grip with jaw and shoulder. Everything depends on balance.

VI. Shoulder hold pizzicato

With the violin held in either of the shoulder holds, place the right thumb on the corner of the fingerboard, slide it down about 2 inches and pluck string with the 1st finger of the *right* hand (fig. 17). (Pupils may try to pluck with the thumb if they have played pizzicato in the under-arm position.)

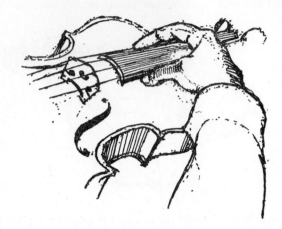

Fig. 17

THE BOW

F. Start by demonstrating the following:

1. How to take bow from case. Use care. Touch the stick but *not* the hair.
2. How to screw up to correct tension for playing. The hair should be about $\frac{1}{2}$ inch away from the stick. (If necessary allow a pencil to pass easily between the stick and hair. This is difficult if the bow is warped. Pupils sometimes ask whether they have a 'Corelli' bow.)
3. How to hold the rosin in its cloth. Apply a little and often, and rub lightly.
4. How to clean the bow stick after playing.
5. How to slacken the bow before putting it away.

(When the bow is not in use it should be placed in the case by the side of the violin.)

The bow hold

The bow is held by the middle finger and thumb, the other fingers serving to balance the bow.

The bow should be held firmly, but so lightly that if flicked by someone it would fly across the room. Fingers should be all curved, and neither jammed together nor spread out too far. The thumb whether straight or bent is often stiff; it should be flexible.

1. *Some drills for bow hold*

(a) Hold bow by middle of stick by the left hand, point to left, heel to right, so that right hand fingers can be arranged at the heel (or nut) of bow.

(b) Right hand. Turn palm upward. Place thumb nail

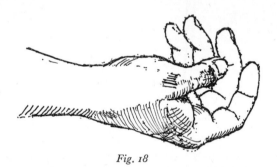

Fig. 18

(the right side of the nail is natural) on the line made at the top joint of longest finger. Keep all loose and bent (fig. 18).

(c) Raise right elbow, turn hand with its back towards you. Now flap the hand backwards and forwards parallel to floor.

(d) Repeat the flapping movement, but with the side of the first finger rubbing the top of the bow stick, anywhere on the stick (fig. 19 overleaf).

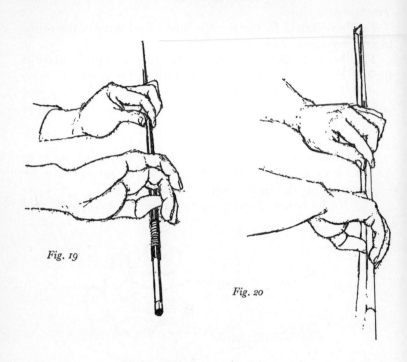

Fig. 19

Fig. 20

(e) Stop movement with hand in sideways position, part the thumb and longest finger just enough to hold the bow stick. The 1st finger should still be on its side on the stick. (fig. 20).

(f) Two fingers are still unplaced. The 3rd finger drops beside the longest finger down to the first joint mark. Place the little finger on its tip just on the near side of the bow stick. It does not curl over the stick as do the other fingers and to place it on the *near* side of the stick rather than the top gives greater ease.

(g) Hold the stick firmly in the left hand and slide the

right hand down to the heel until the thumb touches the black knob of the heel of the bow. The little finger will probably arrive on a line with the mother of pearl spot on the bow (fig. 21). It is a sad moment when a bow is found to be minus its spot.

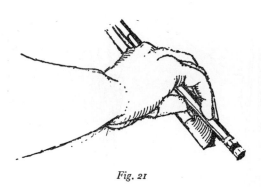

Fig. 21

The first finger is always nearer the point than the thumb; the hand is always slanted and the little finger on its tip.

2. (a) Hold the bow by the middle of the stick in left hand, point to ceiling, nut to floor.
(b) Turn hair towards you.
(c) Drop the right hand from the wrist and place tip of thumb (right side of nail) on stick and against nut (fig. 22 overleaf).
(d) Longest finger round stick opposite thumb.
(e) Drop other fingers round bow stick—little finger on its tip (fig. 23 overleaf).

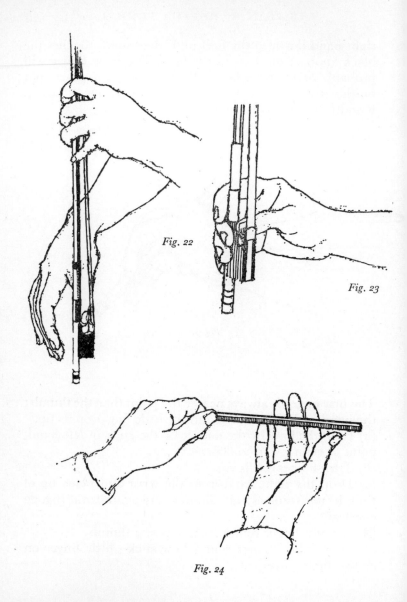

Fig. 22

Fig. 23

Fig. 24

3. *Bow hold drills with a pencil*
   (a) Hold the pencil in left hand.
   (b) Hold right hand up with palm facing you.
   (c) Put the pencil along the top joint marks of 1st, 2nd, and 3rd fingers (fig. 24).
   (d) Put little finger on its tip underneath the pencil.
   (e) Put right side of thumb-nail on to the pencil opposite the 2nd or longest finger. Thumb should be bent and loose (fig. 25).

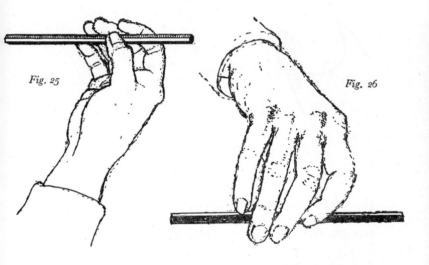

Fig. 25
Fig. 26

   (f) Swivel the right hand slightly so that finger tips point in the direction of the left hand holding the pencil.
   (g) Take left hand away from pencil. Turn right hand over and you should have the right bow hold (fig. 26).
4. *The transfer from pencil to bow*
   (a) Hold the bow screw in the left hand, and the bow horizontally across the body: *hair upwards.*

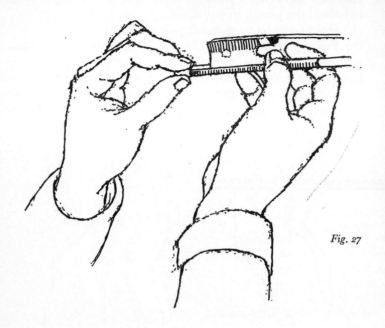

Fig. 27

(b) Imagining that the part of the bow stick nearest the heel is the pencil, do the same drills as in Section 3 but placing the longest finger in the right place on the stick.

5. *Bow arm movements*

(a) Holding pencil as bow, raise right elbow on level with shoulder and push slightly forward.

(b) Move the fore-arm like a hinge, opening and closing; back of hand towards the face and palm away from it. The movement is in front of the body, not at the side.

(c) Drop and raise the upper arm to different heights, and continue the 'hinge' movement.

6. *Bow arm movement, holding bow and resting bow stick on a pencil*

(a) Hold the bow in the usual manner.

(b) With the left hand take hold of one end of the pencil and hold it at arm's length in front of you—pencil upright.

(c) Place bow across left arm, between pencil and your face.

(d) Bend the elbow of the left arm and bring the pencil through the gap between the bow stick and hair and put free end of pencil on your chin. The pencil should be parallel with the floor; the bow stick just touching the

5

fingers. The pencil is now (roughly) where the violin strings will be.

Fig. 29

(e) Keeping the bow at right angles to the pencil, move it from heel to point at various upper-arm elevations corresponding (roughly) with the four string positions. Be careful to make the fore-arm work like a hinge, the elbow coming *forward* towards heel of bow.

(f) Point, heel, middle, down, and up bows can all be tried silently in this way, also different speeds of bowing. For example, four beat bows, two and one beat bows while the teacher plays a tune on violin or piano. See that the bow hold and fore-arm movements are right.

7. *Bow hold manipulative exercises*
    (a) 'Spider' exercise.
    Hold bow correctly, and put it upright in front of you.

(b) Keeping the fingers and thumb as much as possible
in the same relative position, creep up the stick or let the
stick slip through the fingers.

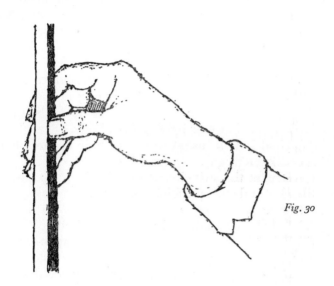

Fig. 30

(c) Creep back again to heel.

8. '*Arc*' *exercises*

(a) Hold bow correctly, but right elbow at side of body,
bow parallel with floor, and across body, with hair
downwards.

(b) Make an arc with the bow by swinging the bow tip
over to the right, with hair turned *upwards*, without moving
elbow away from body.

(c) Swing back again. Keep hand in line with fore-arm.

9. '*Tapping*' *exercises*

(a) Rest bow on pencil (see Section 6).

(b) Hold bow correctly.

(c) Tap each finger of right hand in turn up and down on bow stick.

10. '*Name Writing*' *exercise*

Usual bow hold. With bow upright, at arm's length, pointing to ceiling, 'write' names and words in the air with the tip of the bow, using hand and finger movement only.

11. '*Swivel*' *exercise*

(a) Usual bow hold. Hold bow upright pointing to ceiling and by bending and straightening fingers and thumb roll the stick so that the hair swivels towards the body. Reverse, so that hair is away from body.

(b) Hold bow in usual way with hair towards floor and repeat exercise (a).

(c) Repeat the swivel exercise with bow tip pointing to the *right* and stick parallel with floor.

12. '*Opening Gate*' *exercise*

(a) Usual bow hold. Hold bow across body.

(b) Point the bow to the front, and back again, using hand and fingers only (no arm movement). The action resembles the opening and shutting of a gate.

Notes

While the violin hold and bow hold are being taught, pupils will also attempt tuning and can play open-string pieces (mostly in crotchets), starting with pieces which have the same string repeated several times, followed by those in which the strings have to be crossed more quickly. Rests, repeat marks, and other items of simple notation can be introduced.

Even when playing the simplest open-string pieces, consisting mainly of crotchets, there can be variety of speed, mood, texture and variation of volume of sound. A march followed by a lullaby can convey much, without words, and even pizzicato playing can be used to give a feeling for phrasing by graduating the amount of sound.

Open-string pieces can be good or bad, logical or illogical. If possible there should be a sequence of sounds easily grasped by the pupils. (If the teacher can remember an open-string piece after hearing it twice, it is likely to be good. Otherwise it is possibly too long and illogical in its string sequence.)

When arranging open-string parts to fit a well-known tune, do not be tempted to try and make them more interesting in themselves. An open-string player needs to feel he is playing as much of the tune as possible and keeping the same rhythm as the teacher playing the tune on violin or piano. To take an example: 'Au clair de la lune' is one of many tunes good enough to have phrases repeated.

The same logical sequence can be looked for in original open-string pieces, which are not adapted to well-known tunes.

When shoulder hold and bow hold are reasonably correct, violins can be taken home for practising.

6

STAGE II

A. Placing bow on strings.
B. Bow elevations across strings.
C. Rhythmical movement of bow.
D. Building up of left hand fingering. $0 - 1 - \widehat{23} - 4$
(Pattern I).
    (a) Under-arm hold.
    (b) Shoulder hold.
E. Exercises and tunes. Pizzicato on one string.

It is not always easy for a beginner to get both violin and bow into position at the same time. Here is a suggestion which may help:

    (a) Stand. Face the chair. Place bow across seat of chair, heel to right and hair towards the front of the chair.

    (b) Raise violin to shoulder hold in thumb position. Get pad comfortably adjusted.

    (c) Arrange fingers for bow hold, with bow still on chair. Pick up bow.

    (d) With violin on shoulder and bow in hand, take up correct stance, left shoulder towards charts, head turned, and violin scroll pointing towards charts.

A and B.

    1. (a) Place middle of bow *soundlessly* on D string, half-way between bridge and fingerboard, at right angles to the string.

The right arm should form a right angle at the elbow. This is the 'middle bow' position, and the bow stick on the string is not necessarily at a point half-way between heel and tip. The position differs according to the length of arm.

Fig. 31 (a)

(b) Lift, and place on other strings as the names are called out by the teacher.

(c) Lift, and place middle, heel or point of bow on different strings, as indicated by teacher.

2. (a) Place bow on string D (middle bow).

(b) Without pressure, pull bow lightly to point and return to middle, using forearm 'hinge' movement. Let pupils take their own speed for this.

(c) Pupils continue to bow as in (b). The teacher begins to play a tune, say a march or waltz. After a short time the pupils will bow together at the same speed. The teacher's bow movement should coincide with that of the pupils'. This may be slow at first, but by playing several notes to a bow, a feeling of pulse is introduced. Three notes for a waltz and one, two or four for a match.

The waltz pulse often produces a more relaxed bowing movement.

(d) Pull and push bow, middle to point, on all strings in turn, not always in the usual order (G.D.A.E.). Vary the order.

3. *Whole bows*

(a) Gradually use more and more of the bow until the whole length from tip to heel is used.

(b) Try bowing at full length at different speeds (eight, four, two, one counts to a bow; six or three counts, slow or fast).

4. *Bowing above strings*

(a) Move bow silently and slowly, $\frac{1}{4}$ inch above the strings. This is extremely hard work and pupils find it difficult to use the whole length of the bow.

(b) After a short time allow them to rest the bow on the strings and relax hold on the bow. The relief after 'holding off' gives a feeling of relaxation and the sensation of bowing with a loose hold and no pressure.

5. '*Tops and Tails*'

Place the bow at heel and point alternately at a definite moment. For example:

Count four beats.

First beat. Place bow at heel on string.

Second beat. Lift bow off (it will make a tiny sound) and move to point in the air arriving at.

Third beat. Place bow at point on string.

Fourth beat. Lift, and return in the air to heel for next first beat.

This exercise can be varied in speed.

6.   Down and up bows to dictation. Try to get pupils to

realize that down bows do not always start at the heel, nor up bows at the point.

7. Play whole bows with hair flat on strings. Then swivel the bow stick in the fingers as in Stage I, bow hold drill No. 5, and play on side on bow hair, with hair towards the bridge.

8. Pupils work in pairs for this exercise—

(a) First pupil holds violin in shoulder position and the bow point on any string, at right angles to the string.

(b) Second pupil steadies the bow by holding it under the heel.

(c) First pupil, with hand in bow hold position, strokes the bow stick right up to the point and back again. *The bow itself is not moved.* After making this movement several times, change the bow point to different strings, the heel being held higher or lower by the second pupil as required. If the bow hold is loose, the thumb and longest finger opposite one another, and all other fingers in correct position, the first pupil is given the sensation of drawing a straight bow, and feeling the necessary arm and finger movement at both ends of the bow.

(d) Repeat this exercise, but with second pupil holding the violin and the first pupil steadying the bow.

Bowing drills described in Stage I can still be used, especially those performed with the help of a pencil, or the violin can be turned over and the bow placed on the back of the instrument provided the violin is not a good one. A few moments of silence is sometimes agreeable.

Most of these bowing drills can be done with the violin in the shoulder hold position, and thumb under the body of the instrument. Occasionally, however, the left hand should be placed in the fingering position (see fig. 31(b) overleaf). Teachers find their own words for describing relaxed bow movements. Many liken the hand and finger movement to a large paint brush; the hairs following the strokes of the brush as the fingers follow the hand in the bowing exercises.

'Pull the bow down with the *palm* of the hand, and push up with the back.'—'Can you see the back of your hand as you bow?'—I saw a teacher stick transfers on the back of her pupils' hands, saying 'If you cannot see the picture you are not holding the bow in the right way.' Every teacher will find his own words to express quality of sound. 'Feel as though you are stroking a cat.'—'Sink your bow into half a dozen eiderdowns.' But whatever the words may be, the aim

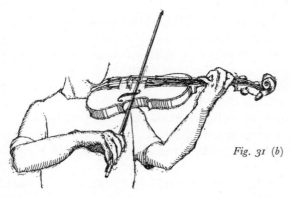

Fig. 31 (b)

is to develop an easy movement of the bow arm and hand, and produce a pleasing sound, avoiding pressure of the bow on the strings.

C. Try to keep bowing drills rhythmical and whenever possible show the notation for 𝅗𝅥 𝅘𝅥. 𝅘𝅥 𝅘𝅥, the notes usually being bowed at this stage. Open-string pieces are now being introduced. Later in this stage, when tunes are played pizzicato with the left hand, the *rhythms* of these tunes can be bowed on open strings.

Greater control and relaxation of bow hold and bowing movement can often be encouraged by holding the bow by different parts of the stick: by the middle, or a third of the way up, or even the point and playing with it upside down.

D. *Left Hand*

Up to now open strings only have been heard, but all pupils realize that other sounds can be produced by pressing the strings on to the fingerboard with the fingers of the left hand, and so altering the length of the string. Many pupils cannot work their fingers independently, and it is sometimes necessary in the early stages to introduce manipulative exercises which have no relation to sound.

Players must be able to move, place, lift or slide a finger just a little before attempting to get correct pitch. Some teachers find it advantageous to fix narrow strips of sellotape to the fingerboard to act as finger-placing marks. If this is done, it must be absolutely accurate for each individual instrument. No printed stick-on-labels are reliable. Another method is to place spots of sellotape or elastoplast on the side of the neck of the violin, and the pupil can see these when playing in the under-arm position. Pencil marks are sometimes used.

I prefer to introduce left hand fingering without these aids. If after two or three lessons muscular control and ear appear to be undeveloped, I sometimes mark the side of the neck with great care. Most of my classes manage without this help. The marks are not frets and the ear still has to be used and the marks are abandoned at the earliest opportunity.

Marks can help in two ways. (a) They enable a pupil to practise manipulative exercises of the fingers in the correct position, and so gain a little mastery over their movements. Touch and feeling are also developed. Attention to pitch is not required at the same moment. (b) All four fingers can be placed on the strings at once, including the little finger, which helps the position of the left hand and avoids that common fault, a collapsed wrist, at a later period.

For many years I did not introduce the 4th finger until later, but I now find that its use helps the position of the left hand. Also it prevents pupils from thinking that the 4th finger is more difficult to use than the others.

If some players have difficulty in reaching the correct position with the 4th finger, let the 1st finger come up, so as to change the weight and balance of the hand to the 3rd and 4th fingers, replacing the 1st finger when necessary. We often have to do this later on, and there is no reason why beginners should not feel this change of balance, and avoid the left hand stiffness which so often occurs, owing to the constant building up with the 1st finger clamped to the string, and probably the left thumb holding up the instrument.

LEFT-HAND DRILLS

1. (a) Sit. Hold violin in under-arm position and take particular care to see that scroll height and angle of violin are correct.

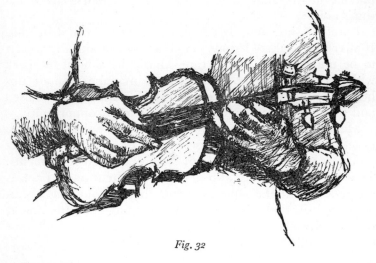

Fig. 32

(b) Place left thumb at right angles to neck of violin, the tip of the thumb level with the fingerboard, about one inch from the end where the strings enter the peg box.

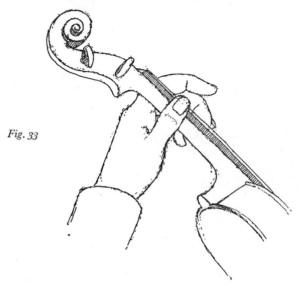

Fig. 33

(c) Rub the side of the base, or bottom joint of the 1st finger, against the other side of the violin neck.

(*Note:* The thumb tip and the bottom joint of 1st finger are the only parts of the hand that should ever touch the neck. The neck should never fall into the V between the thumb and 1st finger.)

(d) Grip the neck hard between the thumb and finger. 'This is the only time in your lives you will do this. NEVER AGAIN.'

(e) Rub lightly again as in (c). Put a finger tip, with nail towards bridge, on any string, and continue rubbing (fig. 34 overleaf).

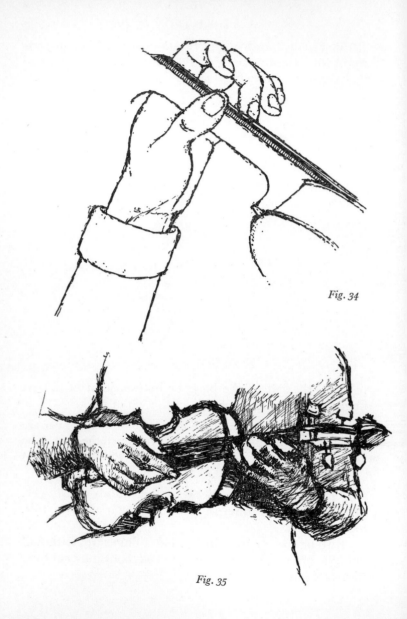

Fig. 34

Fig. 35

(f) As in (e) but with a different finger on a different string.

(*Note :* This is actually a form of vibrato, but here it is used only for hand-loosening.)

2. (a) Under-arm violin hold with left thumb at right angles to neck.

(b) Place all fingers on one string. 1st and 2nd fingers on tips, with nails towards bridge (fig. 35).

(c) Lift all fingers together about an inch off the string, and then put them down again (not necessarily in any finger pattern). Down and up (or press and release) several times. The 'lift' is more important than the placing.

(d) The same exercise as (c) but place fingers alternately on two strings, say A and E, pressing and lifting as before.

(e) The same exercise, but using all four strings.

3. (a) Under-arm violin hold.

(b) Place all fingers as in 2 (b).

(c) Lift each finger up and down in turn, keeping the others lightly on the string.

4. (a) Under-arm violin hold.

(b) Place all fingers as in 2 (b) on a definite string, say A.

(c) Lift each finger in turn and place on D string and back again to A.

(d) Try the other way round, holding on to D string and lifting over to A.

5. (a) Under-arm violin hold.

(b) Put all four fingers down, but with spaces in between.

(c) Lift each finger in turn and place it in different positions, e.g. lift 2nd finger, place it close to 1st finger, lift and place it close to 3rd finger, 'Up, back, up, forward'.

6. The same exercise as 5, but instead of lifting, slide lightly on string with released pressure.

7. (a) Under-arm violin hold.

(b) Place 1st finger on E, 2nd finger on A, 3rd on D and 4th on G, and hold down.

(c) Lift each finger in turn and replace.

8. (a) Under-arm violin hold.

(b) Place fingers on any one string, as near as you can get by visual measurement to Pattern I. 0 – 1 – $\widehat{23}$ – 4.

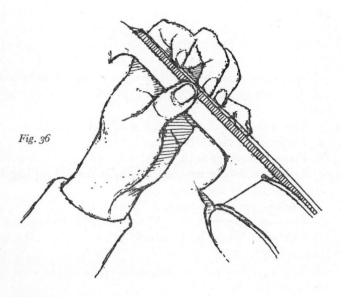

Fig. 36

(c) Lift fingers and replace.

9. This is based on 8. Begin soundless trill exercises of the following type—

(a) 0101, 2121, and repeat;

(b) 0101, 2121, 2323, 4343, etc., calling out the number of the finger as it is put down. The teacher meanwhile plays the sounds, encouraging the pupils to sing the number of the finger if the pitch is suitable. If they cannot be persuaded to sing, it is noticeable that they will alter the pitch of their voices when speaking the numbers. Even more so does this happen when they themselves are playing pizzicato. They may not be able to sing out loud, but one hopes to train them to hear the pitch of the sounds inside their heads.

Notes.

Stress these points. The left hand and arm must be in one line; the thumb up towards the ceiling in shoulder hold, and loose (tap it occasionally on the side of the violin neck); the 1st finger right on its tip with the nail towards the bridge and in the correct manner for playing pizzicato whether using under-arm or shoulder hold. Drills 1 to 9 can also be performed with shoulder hold. Many teachers prefer to do this straight away.

The teacher will find for himself the words which convey most clearly to the class what they are to do. Such words as 'place', 'lift', 'up', 'down', 'over', 'bounce', 'strike', and so on. Whatever they may be, it is important that the words of instruction are given out at even intervals, thus conveying a sense of pulse. The timing may be slow or fast according to the capacity of the pupils, but they must act in unison, not in a haphazard fashion.

There are a number of trick manipulative drills that can be used at this stage and later. For instance an extension of 7 and 8.

10. (a) Under-arm violin hold.
    (b) Thumb in usual position on neck.
    (c) Fingers curled up pressing nails along other side of neck.
    (d) Lift each finger in turn, pluck a string and return it

6

to its position along the neck. Anything in fact that can give strength and independence to the fingers of the left hand.

Drills allied to pitch

Up to now the pupils have used the fingers and have begun to hear the sounds they should produce through the medium of the teacher's playing or by singing. If half the class appears to have much difficulty in doing soundless drills (8) and (9), now is the moment to put marks on the fingerboard or neck of the violin. It will still be necessary to listen intently, but marks may bring the less able pupil a little nearer correct intonation.

When learning to place fingers for pitch it is best to repeat the same sound several times and not play a sequence of single notes at first. This gives a regular pulse, and allows the pupil time to think and hear the sound. Always build up from an open string (even if not quite in tune), for it is the only *steady* sound to which finger placing can be related.

11. *Usual procedure for finger drills with sound*

(a) Under-arm violin hold. Play exercises or drill, pizzicato.

(b) Place all fingers on string again. Stand, keeping fingers down in place. Correct stance.

(c) Still keeping fingers down, move violin to shoulder hold. This helps to avoid collapsed wrists.

12. *A few examples of finger drills with sound*

Before each—

(a) name the string for the exercise.

(b) be sure the first finger is in right relation with open string.

(c) Place all other fingers and check position of left hand.

(d) Lift fingers for exercises.

(e) Call out finger numbers as exercise proceeds.

1. (a) 0000, 1111, 2222, 3333, 4444, and down.
   (b) 0000, 2222, 1111, 4444, 2222, 3333, 1111, 0000.
   (c) 0000, 1111, 2222, 1111, 2222, 3333, 4444, 3333, 4444, 3333, 2222, 1111, 0000.

2. Cut down the number of repeated notes.
   (a) 000, 111, etc.
   (b) 00, 11, 22, 33, etc.
   (c) When you cut down to single notes, there is not time enough to call out the name of the next finger, so make these single note trill exercises short and concise. They can then be learnt by rote 0, 1, 2, 3, 4, 3, 2, 1 and repeat.
   (d) 0101, 2121, 2323, 4343, and backwards 4343, 2323, 2121, 0101, ending with 0.
   (e) 0213, 2431 and repeat.

Drills of this kind can also be done with rests in between each sound thus giving the pupils an opportunity to imagine the sound before they play it. *This is most important* and the same drill can be carried on into the later stages, arco.

Where L H is marked the pupil drops the finger on to the string and imagines the sound—actually hearing it if the fingers are strong enough—then plucks the sound to hear if it is right.

After a time, call out the *names* of the notes, not the number of the finger. (If a ♯ note is played I usually call it by its full name, F♯ or C♯, etc.) In this way the name of the note is related to the finger. Keep to one string for a little while and do not attempt to complete the full scale until later. If the teacher makes sure that all the A's or D's (or whichever string is chosen) are in tune, he can then be adamant about intonation.

During Stage I and the beginning of Stage II the class will have been introduced to the symbols relating to plucking and bowing open string pieces, or time patterns written on charts or blackboard. They have heard the sound of their finger notes and have begun to learn names. This is the moment to start reading pitch. A chart of the following kind is useful:

It will be noticed that this is drill 1 (a).

The pupils have heard the sound, and know the names of the notes, and now they see the notation. A key-signature is written, for which I give no explanation unless questions are asked. Pupils are thinking of a finger pattern; keys come later.

Other drills can be written on different strings.

Having linked sound, name, and notation, start reading backwards, notation – name – sound, and add notes of different values. For example:

E. *And so we come to one-string tunes*

The reason for keeping to one string is that pupils can still play in tune with one open string even if they cannot tune their instrument. Progress will not be satisfactory now unless regular practising begins, and many pupils cannot get help with tuning. Hence the importance of playing in tune on one string. A few examples—all played pizzicato:

As mentioned at the beginning of Stage II in the Bowing Section, the rhythms of these pieces can be bowed on open strings.

7

STAGE III

All sections to run concurrently.

A. Gradual approach to simultaneous use of left and bow hands.

B. { Open string scales and arpeggios (one octave) on G, D and A strings, up and down, pizzicato.
Tunes using all fingers, pizzicato.

C. Rhythmic bowings, different parts of bow, various speeds.

D. Slurs.

E. Tunes (arco), such as folk-songs, hymns, carols.
All 0 – 1 – 2̂3 – 4 pattern.

A. The teacher may find that the use of left and bow hands together may be better introduced in Stage II. It is important to get on with the job, but every class will vary in ability to cover the groundwork. Flagging interest, age of pupils, type of school, etc. will all modify the plan. The teacher will use common sense, but it must be remembered that the more agility and ease of movement gained by each hand separately, the more rapid will be the progress when they are joined together.

1. (a) Posture drill. Shoulder hold. Test finger positions for intonation.

(b) Very simple finger drill. Pizzicato, e.g. 0000, 1111, 2222, etc.

(c) Pick up bow. Check bow hold.

(d) Play finger drill with whole bows. Slowly, counting two to each bow.

2. As in 1, but playing one beat notes with upper half of the bow and then the lower half.

3. Any other finger drills or simple tunes on one string.

Notes

The class will now have begun to cross the strings when plucking open string scales. These scales can now be bowed (even notes).

Pieces and tunes which necessitate crossing the strings may now be chosen for simultaneous fingering and bowing. Many good pieces using only open strings and one finger, or 0 – 1 – 2 can be found. In both cases these fingered-and-bowed pieces should be simpler than the pizzicato tunes being learned, and the rhythms easier than the bowing exercises.

Do not bow *all* tunes plucked previously. If the cost of the music is not prohibitive choose a few new ones. The pupils feel they are learning something fresh, although they are really revising earlier work in a new form. At this point they begin to read notation, bow and finger work together. Later in this stage, however, as the work progresses and becomes more difficult, it is advisable to learn tunes pizzicato; bow the rhythms of the tunes on open strings; and finally put the two together and play in the normal way.

B. *The Left Hand.* (*Started at same time as A*)

1. Scales D, A, G. Pizzicato.

(a) Begin with usual posture and finger-testing drills.

(b) Using the D and A strings, 0 – 1 – 2̂3 produces the

scale of D without using the 4th finger. The open strings
help intonation and there are four sounds on each string.
Play each note twice at the start, and then single notes
up and down. (The difficulty of placing the 3rd finger
coming down should have been helped by getting the
correct position of the left hand in earlier finger drills. I
usually suggest putting the 3rd finger down by itself,
with the others ready to be placed afterwards; not all
fingers down on lower part of string. There is often a
tendency to 'build up' on the lower part of the string,
and this slows the flow of the scale).

2. Scales A and G in the same way as in 1.

3. Arpeggios. D, A, G, keeping fingers down whenever
    possible.

4. Finger drills with particular reference to intervals.
    (a) Broken thirds.

    (b) Broken fourths.

Many teachers find that it is helpful to relate these intervals
to Solfa or the beginnings of well-known tunes, e.g. 'While
Shepherds Watched', 'Poor Old Joe', 'Pop Goes the Weasel'
for thirds; 'British Grenadiers', 'Auld Lang Syne', for
fourths; 'Baa-Baa Black Sheep' for fifths.

Choose and use *one* example only, and stick to it, because
the same reference every time will begin to produce the
sound of the interval in the pupils' minds, and constant use
will make them think the sounds before they play them.

5. Tune playing. Pizzicato.

   (a) Tunes learned by ear, demonstrated by the teacher. The habit of learning by ear can be invaluable for work at later stages, when introducing new fingering.

   (b) Tunes learnt from notation.

Under-arm violin hold is used less and less—shoulder hold more and more.

A few examples of suitable tunes and a short list will be found at the end of the chapter.

C. *Rhythmic Bowings*, using different parts of the bow a different speeds.

   Apart from straightforward bowing exercises, e.g.

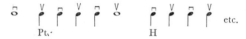

and bowing on open strings the rhythms of pieces being plucked, and joining together left hand and bow, one sometimes needs more advanced exercises still on open strings without the complication of reading difficult notation.

The words of well-known jingles and nursery rhymes can be very useful for this purpose as they often introduce quite complicated bowing rhythms. The teacher should try them out first, and be certain of the words, because odd 'ands' or 'ofs' put in between the lines can upset the placing of the bow.

These exercises are useless unless insistence is placed on the exact part of the bow to be used. Here are some 'fool-proof' nursery rhymes:

1. (a)

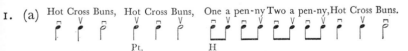

Use whole bow for ♩, half bow (either end as it comes) for ♩, and two or three inches of bow for ♪♪

(b) Same rhythm, starting at the point of bow. ♪♪ will then come at the point of the bow. The tune can be played by the teacher.

(c) On other strings also.

2. (a)

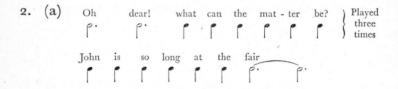

Use whole bow for ♩·, and quarter bow or less for ♩

(b) Begin at point of bow.

(c) Play on other strings.

3. (a)

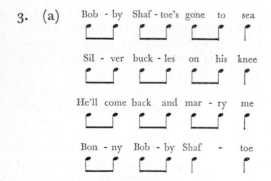

Whole bow for ♩, quarter bow for ♫. Quavers come alternate ends of bow.

(b) Begin at point of bow.

(c) Play on other strings.

4. *Polly put the Kettle on*

The bowing of this tune is almost identical with that of 'Bobby Shaftoe'.

5. *Baa-Baa Black Sheep*

This needs more care if used, and must be slightly altered:

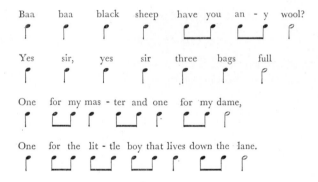

Use whole bow for ♩, slow whole bow for 𝅗𝅥, quarter bow for ♫. The third line needs care, but is obvious when the tune is played. Be careful not to put 'and' between the third and fourth lines; it will upset the bowing. Other tunes can be worked out in the same way.

The tunes can also be played across two strings, but in that event the real tune played by the teacher may not fit. Never play the same string twice running, but see that the same parts of the bow are used as when playing on one string only. For example, 'Hot Cross Buns':

 also start at point

also start at heel

Occasionally (it is rare) one meets the class that can play these across four strings.

D. *Slurs*

These can be introduced across two open strings, ♩ ♩ etc. but the use of fingers and bow together is really implied. Therefore when scales and several tunes have been bowed, slurring may be introduced in the following way:

1. (a) Two notes in one bow. Play any open string, stopping bow half-way and then continuing.

   (b) Using fingers on strings, half bow to each note.

 etc.

(c) Without stopping the bow, play two different sounds, half bow to each note.

(d) Part of a scale, or a complete scale slurred two in a bow.

2. Three notes in a bow.
    (a) As in 1 (a) but divide bow into three.
    (b) As in 1 (b) but three pulses on each sound.
    (c) Play without stopping the bow.

3. Four or more notes in a bow. Generally introduced
    without stops and straight on to half or complete scale.
E. Tunes (arco), folk-songs, hymns, carols.
    All o – 1 – 2̂3̂ – 4 pattern.
1. *Examples of tunes commonly used*
    (a) Twinkle, twinkle, little star. (Sure to be attempted
         by everyone without its being suggested.)
    (b) Cock-a-doodle-do.
    (c) Bells of Vendome.
    (d) Rousseau's Dream.
    (e) Once I loved a Maiden Fair.
    (f) This Old Man.
    (g) Drink to Me Only.
    (h) The Old Woman and the Pedlar.
    (i) Long, long ago.
    (j) J'ai du bon Tabac.
    (k) Here's a Health unto His Majesty.
    (l) Tune from the last movement of Beethoven's Ninth
         Symphony.
    (m) Ye Banks and Braes.
And there are many more. It will be noticed that all the
tunes are within the compass of an octave, and can therefore
be played in the keys G, D, or A, keeping to Finger Pattern I.
    Some tunes, which at first sight seem to fit the finger
pattern, have to be adjusted. For example 'Au Clair de la

Lune', which starts well when played in the key of one of the open string scales:

But the next phrase needs an altered finger pattern and the 3rd finger would have to be ♯ for C♯ or G:

But if the tune begins on the 3rd finger, keys C, G or D (on A) the fingering remains correct, and makes excellent practice for string crossing:

2. *Example of Hymns*

    (a) Duke Street (Fight the Good Fight) S. of P. 298.

    (b) Nicaea (Holy, Holy) S. of P. 187.

            (This often sounds rather drear. Quickly moving tunes are usually more satisfactory.)

    (c) Truro (Jesus shall Reign) S. of P. 545.

    (d) Tallis Ordinal. S. of P. 664.

There are many others. If a particular tune is required and it is not in a key suitable for the players, transpose it. For instance, a popular one: 'Easter Alleluya' ('Let us rejoice,' or 'All Creatures of our God and King'), S. of P. 137, is in E♭. This can easily be transposed to D, but remember that tunes must be within the compass of an octave and two notes, or finger patterns change.

3. *Carols*

    (a) The First Nowell, in D.

    (b) Unto Us a Boy is Born, in D.

    (c) A Child this Day is Born, in D.

    (d) (Dives and Lazarus). Come all you worthy Christian Men. Key E minor; or I heard the Voice of Jesus Say. S. of P. 529.

    (In some editions there is one passing note on A string at double bar. Cut this out).

    (e) The Waits, in G.

4. *Rounds*

    (a) London's Burning, in A.

    (b) Turn Again, Whittington, in D.

    (c) Frère Jacques.

    Scales can also be played in canon.

5. Published violin class 'tutors' usually include many of these tunes. They may also include material for elementary part playing, but this ensemble playing may best be done at some other time than the violin lesson.

8

COMMENTS ON STAGES I, II, AND III

Some of the points mentioned below have been stressed earlier in connection with specific exercises and drills. For the sake of clarity I will risk repetition and include them in this chapter.

1. Classes vary enormously in the time they take to cover the work of these three stages. The average in a Primary School is about a year, but it may well be longer. Quite apart from natural aptitude for the instrument, and the home and school environment, the age of pupils will have great significance. The younger children enjoy doing the same thing again and again, and progress may be slow, but sure. Older children and adults like to get on, but though they grasp the early stages quickly with their minds and their progress may be quick at first, they have difficulty in acquiring new technical skills. Even a detailed plan cannot deal with all the points which may arise during lessons. If questions are asked they should be answered straight away, even if this means abandoning the plan you had drawn up for the lesson. (At the same time one must be wary of the child who asks questions in order to appear bright and interested, but does not really want an answer.)

As a visiting teacher it is often difficult to remember

the questions which have been dealt with in classes at different schools. Keep a note of them in a record book.

2. *Names of parts of the instruments*

There is no need to give a special lesson on these, nor to make a list of parts to be memorized. I speak of them as the instrument is handled. 'Scroll', 'tail-piece', 'pegs', and so on, and by the end of the first term the pupils are usually quite familiar with all the names. The sound-post, for instance, can be spoken of at the end of the lesson before violins are taken home—'Don't swing your violin around or bang it, when taking it home. You may crack it, or the sound-post will fall down.' In the same way the history of the instrument, and the different kinds of woods which go to its making, can be mentioned in answers to questions.

3. *Care of the instrument* (including the use of rosin)

Show the class the way to handle a violin and see that all instruments are wrapped in a soft cloth, and the bow hair loosened before violin and bow are returned to the case. Screwing up and unscrewing of bow hair can be easily taught by drills in class. Wiping rosin off the violin is usually spoken of at the first lesson in which the bow is drawn on the strings; the powder is then quite obvious. The need to rosin a bow 'little and often' can be emphasized by a drill. Now and then, if bows are very devoid of rosin, get the pupils to hold the rosin up in front of the face and do a few bowing drills on it.

The enthusiasm of some young players for putting rosin on bows can be a menace. Imagine a whole class, having completed the drills for posture and bow hold, poised ready to play fingers and bow together. At this moment some 'little innocent' suddenly realizes he has not rosined his bow. Down go his violin and bow, out

7

comes the rosin box, and the whole build-up of the class collapses.

Sometimes I forbid rosining during the lesson, except at the moment of unpacking. If not done then I see that the culprit stays behind at the end of the lesson and does the job correctly.

4. *Notation*

Up to this point the class may think in finger patterns, but questions about clefs, sharps, key and time signatures are sure to have been asked. The pattern of the major scale and the relationship between tones and semitones can best be shown on a keyboard. Young people who start reading music with a violin in their hands find it difficult to realize that E to F, and B to C, are semitones in staff-notation. A piano is usually available and all the pupils can gather round if the class is not a very large one.

Recognition of the sharp keys is easy, as the strings of the violin serve as reminders. G has one sharp, D has two, A has three, and E four, and the last added is the one before the key note. Most people grasp this quite quickly.

Time signatures are sorted out during open-string bowing. It may help if time signatures are written like this at first: $\frac{4}{}$ $\frac{3}{}$ $\frac{2}{}$

Then explain the substitution of a figure for the note:

$$\circ = 1 \quad = 2, \text{ etc.}$$

$\frac{6}{}$ would represent a compound time signature, but there is no need to introduce this until later.

Italian terms can be used from the beginning, even with pizzicato open string pieces: 'When you play these four notes they will get louder and louder—Crescendo; 'Go back to the beginning—D.C. or Da Capo'. There is no need to make lists to be learned. If for some reason, say during examinations in the school building, the class is asked 'not to make a noise', some sort of competition can be held to find out how many of these terms have been remembered. Italian terms for tempo can also be used in the early stages. Because the crotchet was chosen as a suitable pulse note when playing early pizzicato exercises and drills, pupils are apt to think that crotchets are always played at a march speed, and that semibreves are always long sounds. Tunes in the hymn books used for Assembly are puzzling, because although written mostly in minims and semibreves, they are sung and played quite quickly. It must be pointed out that crotchets can be fast or slow, and the relative value of the other kinds of notes remains constant.

Then, of course, comes the question: How can we decide the speed at which a piece should be played? Notice (i) the name of the piece, (ii) the Italian terms (I use a few simple ones such as Allegro, Presto, Adagio, etc.), and (iii) the metronome marks. A metronome has a special fascination for small boys.

5. If a beginner has already learned the piano, he will find it an asset, but it is not essential; indeed, there may be some confusion at first, owing to the numbering of the fingers, four for the violin, and five for the piano. This is only a passing problem which is solved quite quickly, because the violin is such a totally different kind of instrument, and played in a completely different way.

6. *Vibrato*

'Why do you wobble your left hand, Miss?' 'How do you do it?' Two questions asked very often. I try to show the pupils the reason for using vibrato, and explain what should happen to finger and string when playing vibrato. The players may try one or two exercises. (See page 106.) As a rule, curiosity having been satisfied, the subject may be dropped until later, but now and then vibrato can be attempted during the first three stages. Very occasionally one or two pupils may get the sensation quickly.

7. Do not feel compelled to play arco all the tunes that have been learnt pizzicato. Make a note of those which the class seem to enjoy, and use them for bowing. Any others can be regarded as finger exercises.

8. It is sometimes difficult for players to listen to the sounds they make when playing in a group, and a certain amount of individual playing is desirable. Some pupils will listen with interest to others playing, but as a rule it is wise to keep the whole class occupied in a practical way, or thoughts may wander. It is so much easier to hear whether someone else is playing in tune than to hear oneself. Ask a pupil if a note he has played was sharp or flat and he may have difficulty in answering even if he has a good ear. Ask the rest of the class and almost anyone will answer without hesitation.

Listening, pure and simple, must be done occasionally, but if individuals are to be heard it is best to ask the rest of the class to play pizzicato while the soloist uses the bow, or to play phrases in turn, all joining in the last phrase. This keeps the class alert and concentrating on the matter in hand. Teachers will devise many ways of encouraging pupils to listen; the non-existent radio set playing in the distance, a clock, a train whistle, or, if a pianist, ask the class to listen for a hidden tune, but on the whole try to apply listening to intonation or quality of fiddle tone.

9. Although I advocate keeping the left and right hands separate in the early stages, I know perfectly well that children will try to play 'Twinkle, Twinkle' with bow and fingering as soon as they pick up an instrument,

particularly when it goes home for practising. I would not dream of stopping this—long may pupils want to try things for themselves—but I want to make sure in the first lessons that everything is as well done as it possibly can be.

10. *Music for Classes*

My pupils are usually asked to buy two books for the first three stages.

(a) *One of the many books published for violin classes—so-called 'tutors'.* I change from one to another with different classes—all have merits and a few drawbacks. Most of them contain fingering and bowing exercises, and, what is more important, a number of traditional tunes and adapted songs of the types listed in Stage III.

(b) *A book of pieces for beginners*

These usually contain open-string pieces followed by others which introduce one finger at a time, 0 – 1, 0 – 1 – 2, and 0 – 1 – 2̂3. These supply open-string material for the first lessons, and later simple pieces for fingers and bow together. They are often more truly instrumental in quality than adapted songs.

If extra material is needed, it may be necessary to write MS copies of a hymn or carol. To ask the class to copy a tune down from the blackboard might take all the time in a lesson, and the copying is not always reliable. So in the early stages I write these myself or duplicate copies. If MS is used I suggest a large supply of paper clips or sellotape, so that the slips of MS can be attached firmly to the inside of printed music books, or an exercise book kept for the purpose. MS may be pasted in the exercise book, but pupils forget to do this, and the result is a number of crumpled and torn scraps of paper which will not stay on a violin stand. Clips or sellotape offer the most satisfactory results.

11. *Group playing* of some kind should be encouraged at this stage, if possible, apart from ordinary class-work. Opportunities for this may arise naturally. There may be a school orchestra which members of the class may be allowed to attend on some special occasion. If they join in the playing of one or two pieces the pupils must be furnished with carefully edited parts.

Then there is the playing of a hymn for Assembly, or attendance at a festival or playing day.

If there are no opportunities such as these, it may be possible to arrange a few sessions to which parents might be invited to hear a demonstration of the way in which the violin is being learned in class, and give them a bird's eye view of work already done.

9

STAGE IV

A. Finger Pattern o – 1̂2 – 3 – 4 (Pattern II).
    (or scale beginning on 3rd finger).
    Scales and arpeggios C—1 octave starting with 3rd finger
                                     on G.
                         G—1 octave starting with 3rd finger
                                     on D.
B. Bowings. Consolidation of Stage III.

In setting forth a plan for teaching it seems necessary to
divide it into sections or stages, but these stages are not
complete in themselves, and will overlap one another.

The introduction of Pattern II may well take place while
work continues in Stage III.

In an effort to make intonation more certain in Pattern I,
one is tempted to leave the introduction of a new pattern too
long, and fingers arrange themselves in Pattern I auto-
matically. At least part of each lesson during the later part
of Stage III should be devoted to pizzicato drills in the new
finger pattern (Pattern II).

It is advisable to start new patterns at the beginning of a
term, and not just before the holidays.

A. Drills will probably be done with violin in shoulder-hold
    position.

1. (a) Place four fingers in Pattern I.

(b) Lift 2nd finger and place it next to 1st finger.

(c) Lift 2nd finger and place it back close to the 3rd finger.

(Placing the 2nd finger next to the 1st finger may produce stiffness. Let the little finger come up if necessary.)

2. Pizzicato drills as in Stage II in Pattern II;

0 − 1̂2 − 3 − 4.

3. Names of the new sounds.

4. Pizzicato scale G. One octave. Starting with 3rd finger on D.

Pizzicato scale C. One octave. Starting with 3rd finger on G.

5. Same scales arco.

6. Playing tunes by ear. Pizzicato.

(Tunes already well-known in Pattern I. The nursery rhyme (Twinkle, Twinkle) is used first, in G, top octave, and C, lower octave.)

7. Same tunes arco.

8. New tunes in Pattern II. Pizzicato and arco.

It will depend on the age and ability of pupils what type of tune is chosen for this new material. Pieces instrumental in character can be found in published works, or traditional songs and hymns can still be used. It is advisable to choose according to finger-patterns and not the keys, for it will be found possible to play pieces in keys other than C (lower octave) and G (top octave). Sometimes, for instance, a modulation will keep finger patterns correct, e.g. key C: a modulation into G with accidental F♯ on E string,

etc.

or in F on lower strings, crossing to A and E provided there
is no 1st finger note.

Traditional songs and hymns are not always found in
suitable keys, and MS transpositions will be needed. Many
of the best hymn tunes are either in keys difficult for elementary players or have one accidental which upsets the 'pattern'.

Here are two examples: (i) Darwell (S. of P. 701) in
C Major. A fine strong tune often sung at Assembly, but
there is one wretched F♯ on D string which necessitates
moving the position of the 2nd finger. (ii) St. Anne (S. of P.
598) has the same difficulty.

The only thing one can do is to push on to the next stage
as quickly as it is safe to do so.

A great tune which conforms to Pattern II, and seems
attractive to every class, is the Passion Chorale (S. of P. 128),
Bach.

An interesting example of a folk-song suitable at this stage
is 'My Love's an Arbutus'. Played in Key G there is no F♯
on D string in spite of all other notes being played on that
string.

B. *Bowing. Consolidation of Stage III*

1. Practice of broken slur and legato slurs continues. Even tone throughout length of bow (not weakening at the point).

2. New rhythm for scale playing. The traditional longer key note is introduced. ♩♪♪♪♪♪♪♩ alternate ends of bow, and also with slurs.

3. Slurred arpeggios.

4. Two-string, open string bowings as in Stage III.

5. Greater consideration of tone variety produced by management of bow.

(a) Up to now f's and p's etc. have been obtained mostly by the amount of bow used; much bow for loud playing, little for soft.

(b) Now use a flat bow (much hair), or hair turned towards bridge (little hair).

(c) Point of contact on string. Near bridge or near fingerboard. (By intent, and not by chance as so often happens if the bow is not straight.)

6. Arco and pizzicato. Alternate between the two, holding the bow while plucking the string. The change from bow hold to plucking hold can be a useful manipulative exercise.

10

STAGE V

Combination of Finger Patterns I and II.

$$0 - 1 - \widehat{23} - 4$$
$$0 - \widehat{12} - 3 - 4$$

A. 1. *Major Scales and Arpeggios*
      G. Two octaves.
      D. Extended to E string (but no C♯ on G string).
      C. Extended to G string (but no F♮ on E string).
      F. On G and D strings only.
  2. *Minor Scales*
      G. D. A. One octave, melodic, upwards only.

B. *Bowings*
Uneven speeds of bow movement. Legato and broken slurs. Uneven slurs, staccato, martelé, slow spiccato and smooth bow.

By this time it is probable that pizzicato for note-learning is unnecessary. It is used for musical effect, or for very tricky intonation when thinking of finger placing. Constant string-plucking does not produce a very pleasant sound, and it is extremely difficult to hear whether intonation is correct. The under-arm hold is no longer used.

A. *Left Hand*
The main concern is the placing of the 2nd finger in two

different positions across the strings, sometimes close to the 1st finger; sometimes close to the 3rd. For example, in Key G, F♯ on D and C♮ on A.

1. The scale G major in two octaves is the basis for this stage and can be explained
   (a) Open string scale followed by 3rd finger scale, or,
   (b) Pattern I on G and D. Pattern II on A and E.
   (How blithely some pupils will continue on the E string to note A without listening or thinking of what they are doing! One hopes to have inculcated a feeling for a keynote by this time, but the fingers will run on if the player is not concentrating.)

2. Within the limits of these two finger patterns, other scales should be played and extended. I have met young violinists who do not realize it is possible to play on the G and E strings in the key of D because the scale has always begun on D open string to D 3rd finger on A; so extend your scales.
   For example:

To continue on to G string involves another finger pattern, so leave it for the moment, but pieces could be played in D on G string provided C♯ is not used.

conform to Pattern I

3. In the same way other keys can be used:
   C with no F♮ on E but all notes on G, D and A

F on G and D and the other strings provided there is
no B♭ or F♮ on A and E.

4. *Minor Scales*. G, D and A, one octave, melodic form
upwards only.

$$0 - \widehat{12} - 3, \quad 0 - 1 - \widehat{23}$$

5. *Finger Drills*. Dominant sevenths, starting on open strings,
can be most useful for the placing of the 2nd finger
without help from the others.

6. Arpeggios co-ordinated with scales, measuring finger
placing across the strings.

7. Finger drills for greater control and agility. Dotted
rhythm, or grace note trill exercises with help to indivi-
dualize the fingers and cultivate the quick lift.
   (a) Fingers down on A string in Pattern I or II.
   (b) Play on D soundlessly or arco.

8. Broken thirds as in Stage III and any other trill exercises.
It will be realized how important it is at this stage that
finger patterns and keys are being related.

B. *Bowings*
   At this stage it is essential to use bow and fingers of left

hand together for bowing exercises. It is no longer possible to segregate bowing movements from fingering and use open strings. The more usual elementary bowing studies are not really suitable for violin class work. They are often long and involve much unnecessary note learning. Time is better spent on note learning of pieces. So practise bowings on scales or short themes which can quickly be learned from memory.

Themes can be presented to the class, or the pupils can be encouraged to write them for themselves. It is usual to give careful definite directions, for instance 'Four bars in $\frac{4}{4}$ time, Pattern I (or Pattern II or I and II together) crotchets all the way unless a long note is needed at the end.'

The tunes are produced at the next lesson. It is advisable for the teacher to play them, to do them justice. The class then chooses one or two of the tunes as the bowing themes to be learnt during the term.

A theme in $\frac{4}{4}$ time is the most useful as a rule, but one in $\frac{3}{4}$ or $\frac{6}{8}$ may be necessary for the second half of the term.

Here are one or two examples written by children in a Primary School.

There is nothing very exciting or original in these tunes; they are ordinary and straightforward, but that is just what is wanted. They must be simple and easy to remember, so that although fingers are being used, it is possible to concentrate on bowing movements.

The bowings usually introduced at this stage can be played on scales, but with these themes the rhythm of the notes can be changed. Four bars can be quickly copied and easily memorized.

The bowings should be chosen as preparation for pieces which will be learned later. Here are three or four examples on themes 1 and 4.

(a) *Slurs*
On theme 1.

On theme 4.

(b) *Broken slurs*

(c) *Uneven speeds of bow movement.* The rhythm of the themes can be changed if necessary. Try to keep even tone on uneven notes.

(d) *Uneven slurs*. Broken slurs stopping bow on dot.

(e) *Martelé* bowing. Usually in upper half of bow on the string, pinching bow stick on to the string in the rest, and releasing pressure as soon as the bow moves and the sound is played,

or on theme 4.

Pupils can sometimes be helped to feel the sensation of this press-release bow movement by suggesting that the thumb should press upwards and not the first finger downwards. It comes to the same thing in the end.

(f) *Slow spiccato*. Lower part of the bow, near heel, and coming off the string,

or on theme 4.

(g) *Smooth bow changing*. As for slow spiccato, but *on the string* at heel, middle or point of bow.

Semiquavers and demisemiquavers can be written to introduce the notation for (e) (f) or (g).

(h) *Some other agility bowings.*

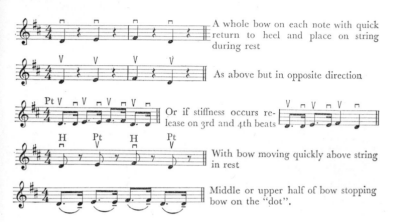

A whole bow on each note with quick return to heel and place on string during rest

As above but in opposite direction

Or if stiffness occurs release on 3rd and 4th beats

With bow moving quickly above string in rest

Middle or upper half of bow stopping bow on the "dot".

It is helpful to try all these bowings with the bow held in different parts of the stick. Martelé bowing and hand movement for change of bow can also be encouraged by resting the right elbow on a table or ledge. The speed or slowness of a travelling bow may well be considered at this stage and pupils can be shown how speed of bow can affect quality of tone and colour and how this has to be adapted to the musical content of a piece.

Printed music for this stage is not difficult to find. Traditional tunes and some of the greatest hymn tunes can now be played, but although there is a great wealth of these, pupils do not (and should not) want to play continually songs adapted for the violin. Try to find pieces that are truly instrumental in character, although they may be quite elementary.

STAGE VI

Sharp Scales

A. 1. Finger pattern 0 – 1 – 2 – ͡34 (Pattern III) or scales and arpeggios starting on 1st finger, one tone from open string.

      Scale B starting with 1st finger on A⎫
        ,,   E   ,,   ,, ,, ,,   ,,   D⎬ one octave
        ,,   A   ,,   ,, ,, ,,   ,,   G⎭

    2. Scale A. Two octaves (Patterns I and III)
       ,,   D extended across four strings (I, II, III)
    3. Scales B, E, A melodic *minors* one octave (I, II, III)

B. Bowings. Consolidation of Stage V.

With care and determination one may get reasonable posture and free bowing from violin class pupils, but really good intonation can be a major problem. For this reason I have based all future stages on left-hand finger patterns and keys, attempting to introduce each separately and gradually joining them together.

As already noted in the 'Outline', most class teachers use finger patterns I and II in the early stages of violin class work, but after this there is much variation in the order in which the patterns are presented. Any order may be adopted as long as the fingerings are taught in logical sequence.

I chose finger-pattern o – 1 – 2 – ͡34 – (Pattern III with sharpened 3rd finger) to follow patterns I and II as I found so many elementary orchestral pieces and arrangements introduced the sharpened 3rd finger, especially in 2nd violin parts. Also the first two scales for violin in most national examinations were G in two octaves and A in two octaves. Although each fingering is taught separately, there is no need to keep them apart for long. Pupils have already used mixed finger-patterns, and each fingering should be linked as soon as possible with those learned previously.

Bowing is developed on the new scales, or more advanced bowing themes, according to the needs of pieces, which in turn are chosen in the appropriate new keys.

A. *Left Hand*
   1. Major scales and arpeggios. B, E, A, one octave, introducing the new sharpened placing of the 3rd finger (Pattern III).
   2. Tunes by ear, already learned, such as 'Twinkle, Twinkle'. Finger drills as in previous stages.
   3. (a) Even trill exercises at different speeds.
      (b) Broken thirds in suitable keys.
      (c) Dotted or grace note trill exercises as in Stage V.
   Finger patterns have already been mixed and Pattern III can soon be linked with I and II. This leads to playing
   4. A. Scale and arpeggios. Two octaves (I and III)
   5. D.   „   „   „   extended across all four strings (Patterns I, II, III)
   6. B.E.A. „   „   „   melodic *minors* one octave (I, II, III)

Scales can all be played with
   (a) Even notes, separate bows
   (b) The usual rhythm of waiting on the key note

    (c) Slurs for (a) or (b)

    (d) Any other bowings.

Arpeggios can be played with separate bows or slurred.

    The main concern in this stage is the placing of the 3rd finger in its two different positions across the strings—close to the 2nd finger or close to the 4th finger.

    Again the dominant seventh can be of help, starting on the 1st finger.

 and on other strings.

Chromatic movement can be made at this stage (if not earlier) but always measured from the anchored 1st finger or 2nd finger.

The finger must move with great speed and lightened pressure on the string.

B. *Bowing*

    Some of the many bowings suggested in Stage V will have been learned, and these can now be consolidated. The others can be taught during Stage VI. In order to gain more agility it is useful to have a scale-type finger exercise for the bowing theme.

    One of the recognized classic finger exercises can be used—for example:

Or an exercise which crosses two strings—for instance:

A great variety of bow movements can be attempted. Start ⊓ or V: play the exercise at heel, middle, or point of bow. And there are an infinite number of slurs and rhythms. Here are some examples:

It is still important not to teach different kinds of bowing for bowing's sake, but to introduce them when they are needed for a piece which is being learned.

12

COMMENTS ON STAGES IV, V, AND VI

Learning to play a musical instrument is not an even, steady, upward process. Progress is not always apparent; indeed there are times when it seems to cease altogether. In my own scheme of class work I have noticed that one of these periods occurs during the teaching of Stages V and VI. The excitement of beginning is over, and playing the violin is proving far harder work than had been expected. Some pupils begin to give up hope of making headway, and teachers to wonder why they chose a profession for which they are obviously unfitted. This is the time for the teacher to accept the challenge and use every possible ingenuity to create incentives which will lift the class over this hurdle.

Ensemble playing and playing days will help, and adjudications may be stimulating, but to play in an orchestra is the best incentive. From the point of view of learning to play the violin use any technical novelties which are particularly suited to the violin and which will catch the fancy of the players and act as an incentive. Theory of Music, Notation, and many technical matters can be turned to account, and may best be noted here and not left until the end of the detailed plan.

It is at this time, too, that classes may need to be

reorganized or divided according to ability and power of self-discipline.

The more talented pupils should not be held back. It is possible that a few less able or less interested pupils will leave the class, and one always hopes their short experience of playing an instrument will have widened their interest in music.

Theory and Notation

No one expects a child to read or write before it can speak. In the same way a young instrumentalist must have some vocabulary before he can read or write music, but the time comes when he must begin and have some knowledge of the written symbol.

It will be realized from the keys in which pupils are playing and the notation used, that some understanding of theory and notation is essential. Up to Stage IV pupils may have thought in finger patterns only, but now it is necessary that they should be familiar with the pattern of the major scale and arpeggios; recognize key signatures, time signatures, and to know what the signs ♯, ♭, or ♮ do to a sound.

It is to be hoped that some of this work will be covered in the general music lessons in the school, but in nearly every class, whether of children or adults, there are gaps in the understanding of these things. Some violin pupils have already had piano lessons, but for many the violin class brings the first introduction to written music. This is the moment to make sure the players understand some simple rudiments of music, and a certain amount of written work may be necessary.

One of the many published exercise books on rudiments can be helpful, but there is no necessity for actual theory lessons if theory and notation have been applied to violin playing in all the early stages. As already mentioned at the end of Stage III, questions will often make it possible to solve difficulties. There are ample opportunities and the rule should be

    (1)   'Watch and listen'

    (2)   'Now do it yourselves'

    (3)   'This is how it is written down'

The order in which these matters are introduced will vary enormously from class to class, and will depend on the exercises and pieces being learned.

Ear-training for pitch, interval, and quality of tone should always be borne in mind, but it is so often neglected for manipulation and note learning. This is my reason for teaching so much by ear. Theory and notation are only incidental in the early stages, but now certain rudiments must be understood and always related to playing.

Vibrato, and some musical incentives

Vibrato. The movement may have been attempted earlier, but probably as a manipulative exercise, or to appease curiosity. Now is the time to make the first real effort to produce vibrato. The necessary movements and sensations come quickly and easily to some pupils, whereas others may take a very long time to achieve satisfactory results. Vibrato, of course, will never come if the left hand is stiff. It may be for this reason that adults usually find it more difficult than children to acquire the skill necessary to produce a good effect.

It is one of those things which must be tried and dropped, tried and dropped. Some teachers consider intonation must be absolutely safe before vibrato is attempted, but I believe it to be an intrinsic part of string playing and that it helps to give sensitivity to the fingers of the left hand. Also pupils are greatly encouraged in their work if they can produce a tone of better singing quality, and for these reasons I introduce exercises for acquiring vibrato at an early stage. This does not mean that (if I can help it) pupils are allowed to use it indiscriminately. We play with and without vibrato. Few of us would ever use vibrato if we insisted on 'every note being dead in tune before we vibrate' or that 'Scales must never be played with vibrato'. Judicious use of the movement as early as possible is my aim. There is some controversy as to whether arm, hand, or finger vibrato should be taught first, but this seems to me of little consequence. Let the pupil choose that which comes most easily and naturally, and the other forms can be cultivated later.

It is difficult to teach a sensation, but this is what has to be done. The note has to be sharpened and flattened and the teacher must watch carefully for signs of sham vibrato, as for instance when the finger releases the pressure on the string instead of rolling on it.

Here are some exercises for giving the feeling of vibrato.

Without using an instrument

1. Hold left arm up in playing position. Flap the hand towards the face and then away. A small movement and quite quick. Keep the fingers very loose, and suggest the tips of the fingers should feel heavy.

2. (a) Clasp the left thumb lightly with the right hand (fig. 37 overleaf).
   (b) Place the tips of the left-hand fingers down the centre back of the right hand, fingers pointing downwards to right wrist (fig. 38 overleaf).
   (c) Massage the right hand with the left fingers, feeling the bones as the finger tips move the skin on the hand.

Exercises with the instrument

3. (a) Under-arm hold
   (b) Place fingers on D string and massage as in (2).

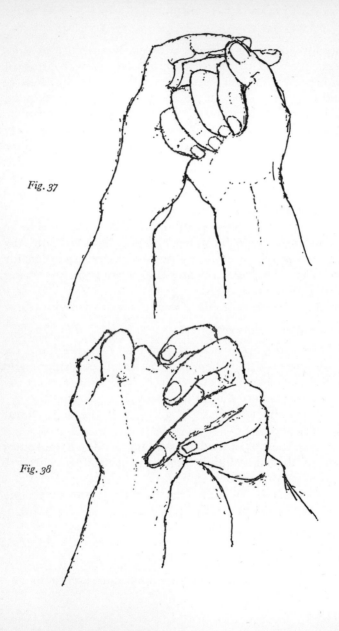

Fig. 37

Fig. 38

Thumb away from the neck at first, then thumb lightly against the neck.

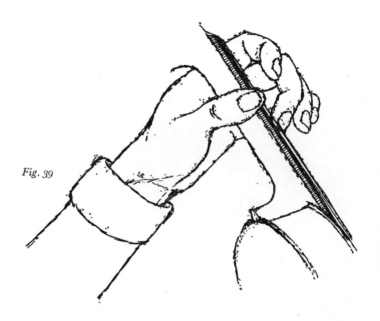

Fig. 39

4. (a) Under-arm hold.
(b) Place the 2nd finger on the string by itself. (Most people seem able to vibrate most easily on 2nd finger.)
(c) Roll the finger tip as though sharpening and flattening the sound, keeping the finger balanced high on its tip for the sharpened position and allow it to flatten a little by rolling on the pad of the finger for the flattened sound.
(d) Repeat the exercises with other fingers.

5. Repeat Exercise 4 with a regular pulse rhythm ♩♩♩♩, and then at double speed, ♫♫ ♫♫.

6. Shoulder hold. (If necessary hold the violin with the right hand, or against a wall for steadiness.) Repeat Exercises 3, 4, 5, in this position. It may help to hold the left elbow up with the right hand or place the elbow on a table or ledge. This seems to release any stiffness in the left arm.

Fig. 40

7. Shoulder hold.
   (a) Place 2nd finger high up on G string (about note E).

The thumb will be where the neck joins the body of the violin.

(b) Massage the string in this position, first sharp, then flat.

(c) Try (a) and (b) using other fingers.

The hand is against the violin and can produce a hand or wrist vibrato.

8. Using the positions and exercises given previously, repeat, but with *two* fingers on strings, always trying to feel the weight and balance of the hand behind and over the fingers being used.

9. Sometimes the sensation of vibrato can be developed by allowing the left hand to be in a bad position, although this is sometimes dangerous. The left wrist, instead of being in a line with the arm, can be held in or out in a slightly exaggerated manner. Always stress feeling with the finger tips and weight balanced over the finger.

10. There are many drills—almost stunts—advocated by some teachers, or 'schools' of violin playing, to introduce the vibrato movement, for instance:

(a) Stand. Violin shoulder hold.

(b) Place scroll on seat of chair.

(c) Try vibrato movement (see fig. 41 overleaf).

Some of these drills necessitate standing almost on the head, but such gymnastics can be helpful in giving the relaxed sensation required. It is important to remember, however, that what can be done with an individual pupil may well develop into a riot in the class-room. These drills have to be presented with discretion and without losing the true interest and discipline of the class.

When you see a vibrato movement made reasonably well by a member of the class, use your own bow, and bow the string for him. This may help the pupil to hear more clearly

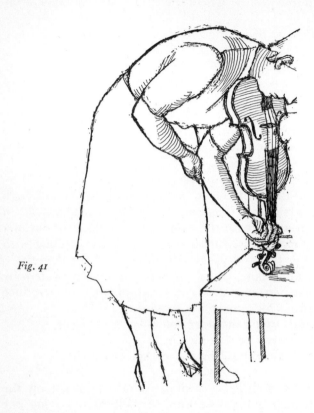

Fig. 41

what he is doing, but on many occasions he collapses with laughter.

When bowing is introduced, the right hand may want to make the same movements as the left, and a scratchy tremolo may be the result at the first effort, but this difficulty is soon overcome.

Other incentives

1. *Chord Playing*

  (a) Cadences of this type can be used:

  (b) A progression of sounds based on simple chords can be taught by ear, the whole class learning all melodic lines. These melodies can then be combined and used as a harmonic background to well-known tunes. The notes are simple; intonation, balance of sound, and sensitivity in accompaniment will need special consideration.

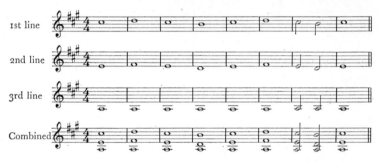

These chords can provide an accompaniment for such tunes as:-

2. *Arpeggio passages* across four strings on simple chording. This sounds quite grand but is not unduly difficult. Upper half of bow or move quickly very near point.

D.C.

3. *Harmonics* (natural)

What they are. How they work. How they are written down.

(a) ½ string. Octave sound.

(b) ¼ string. Two octaves (both ¼ distance from bottom of the string or ¼ distance from the top).

(c) ⅓ of string.

4. *Simple double stopping*, with open string as one of the notes.

(a) Each note separate and then joined

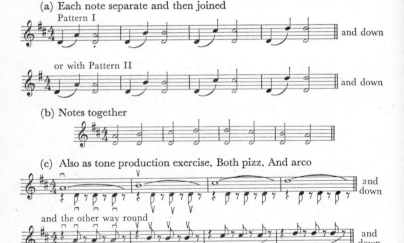

(d) Repeat on two other strings as well.

The training of the ear to hear intervals of sixths, sevenths, and octaves is an obvious outcome of these exercises.

5. *Left hand pizzicato* in its simplest form, with bow playing on another string.

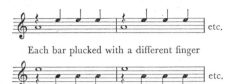

Each bar plucked with a different finger

6. *Composing tunes*

In my experience it is rare to find a violin pupil, young or old, who wishes to compose tunes, but occasionally the idea will act as an incentive. If you ask for an original tune straight away you are apt to get impossible compositions which are sheer waste of time, but by presenting something on which a tune can be based, quite interesting work may be produced.

The idea of a bowing theme by each member of the class has already been suggested (see page 96). This rather cut and dried idea can be presented in a more imaginative form. For instance, in a Primary School I gave some rhythmic dictation in a lesson. I played a tune in short phrases, and after clapping each phrase the pupils made an attempt to write down the rhythm on one note. This was the result:

This was to be taken home and turned into a tune they could play on their violins. It was to have a key signature and any Italian terms they cared to use, expression marks and bowings.

9

A fortnight was the time allowed for this, and I would play the tunes to the class, and perhaps, if any were good enough, they might be played at the concert.

All ten children in the class produced a tune. The four below were chosen by the class as the best for the concert, and a parent of one member of the class volunteered to write piano accompaniments. The composer played it as a solo, and the whole class joined in when it was repeated.

1. Derek. Aged 9.

2. Margaret. Aged 10.
   This child had no piano at home and I always wondered how she got the modulation without (as far as I know) any harmonic background.

3. Jean. Aged 10.

4.   Anthony. Aged 9.

Nos. 1 and 3 are ordinary. Nos. 2 and 4 are more unusual, and the jump of an octave at the end of No. 4 makes the tune, but Anthony was an unusual child. He suffered from ill-health and constantly missed lessons. His mother often came in his stead and took notes and reported back to him, even when he was in bed.

There may not be the time or opportunity to use the suggested incentives at this stage. In that case they may well be carried over to Stages VII, VIII and IX.

13

STAGE VII

Flat Scales

A. Finger pattern ⌢0̂1 – 2 – ⌢3̂4 (or Pattern III flat)
    Scales start on 1st finger, ½ tone from open string.
    1. B♭, E♭, A♭   one octave
    2. B♭   two octaves
       A♭   two octaves
    3. Extended scale F, starting at F on D string up to
       B♭ on E string, but *not* lower on D and G strings.
    4. Scales in sixths.
B. Bowing. Continuation of Stage VI.

It will be noticed that the finger pattern for this stage is exactly the same as in Stage VI, but made flat.

Watch the position of the left hand very carefully as there is a tendency to allow the left wrist to come up as the fingers go back.

Stress the point that the 1st finger must still remain on its tip, and, if anything, this finger is more doubled up than before, and the whole hand can be taken backwards.

A. *Scales and Finger Exercises*
    1, 2, and 3, will be introduced as in earlier stages, that is,

(a) Scales, arpeggios and dominant sevenths and finger
drills in the new pattern, and

(b) tunes the class already plays by ear.

Besides attempting to find published works for pieces in
this fingering it is sometimes useful to write MS folk tunes in
the pentatonic scale. In this way the flattened position of the
hand is introduced without the flattened open string note.
For example 'Ye Banks and Braes' in B♭.

The flattened 4th finger is, of course, an intrinsic part of the
flat scales, but the use of the pentatonic scale at this moment
will give pupils one less thing to think about, besides sound-
ing lovely in itself.

4. Double stopping. Scales in sixths.

These are the only double-stopping scales that do not require
position work. I choose E♭ and B♭ first because they are the
only ones which need no changed finger position across the
strings. Each finger is placed on both strings in the same
pattern.

This may prove a more satisfactory moment to introduce
the double-stopping tone exercise mentioned in Stage V.

B. Bowings as in Stage VI.

14

STAGE VIII

A. 1. *Finger Patterns* (a) ⌢01 – 2 – 3 – 4 (Pattern IV)
              (b) 0 – 1 – 2 – 3 – 4 (,,   ,,)
     Exceptions to the four basic finger patterns
    2. Minor Scales.
    3. Chromatic Moves.
    4. Double-stopping, scales in sixths, in first position.
B. Bowing.
C. Theory and Notation.
D. Other incentives.
    Stages VII, VIII and IX (Position Work) are frequently
    interchanged, combined and telescoped. Indeed, at this
    point it is almost impossible to define the stages clearly.
    Much of the material suggested for use in stages VII and
    VIII is more difficult than actual position work in
    Stage IX.

A.
1. Finger pattern (a) ⌢01 – 2 – 3 – 4   (Pattern IV)
        or (b) 0 – 1 – 2 – 3 – 4 (,, ,,)
   (a) Used in key C on E string
        ,, ,, ,, F ,, A ,, (if open string E is not used)
        ,, ,, ,, B♭,, D ,, (,, ,,   ,, A ,, ,, ,,)
        ,, ,, ,, E♭,, G ,, (,, ,,   ,, D ,, ,, ,,)

(b) Used in key B on G and D strings, or in other keys if open strings are avoided.

This stage has no closely related complete scale, it is used for filling gaps in keys. The main concern is the placing of the 1st finger in its two positions across the strings, from the semitone-from-open-string to the tone-from-open-string, necessary in keys F and C when crossing all four strings. Up to this point the 1st finger has always been placed across all four strings in the same position whether a tone or a semitone from the open string, and all other fingers have been measured from it.

Now the last anchorage has gone—

In major scale work, I make great use of extended scales in the keys listed in (a) and (b) above.

Exceptions to the four basic finger patterns

2. Minor scales and arpeggios

    (a) G. D. A. Harmonic. One octave. (Introduces 1½ tone placing 6̂1 – – 2̂3)

    (b) G. D. A. Melodic. One octave

    (c) A. E. B. Harmonic. One octave (Introduces 1½ tone placing 0 – 1̂2 – – 3̂4)

    (d) A. E. B. Melodic. One octave. (Already introduced in Stage VI)

    (e) G. A. B. Harmonic Minors. Two octaves.

    (f) G. A. B. Melodic Minors. Two octaves.

3. Chromatic scales

    (a) G. D. A. One octave

    (b) Some first position two octave scales.

    (c) Finger drills for agility of finger placing.

        (1) 12, 1 – 2, 1 – – 2, 1 – – – 2, and even 1 – – – – 2.

        (2) Starting with 2nd finger in third position (it does not matter whether the pupils know they are playing in that position.)

21, 2 — 1, 2 — — 1, 2 — — — 1, and perhaps 2 — — — — 1.

    (3) Between other fingers—stretching and step-
ping.

All scales and arpeggios and chromatic can be played
with the usual varied bowings.

4. Double-stopping scales

    In sixths, key note at top.

    (a) F one octave. 1st finger changes its position across
the strings.

    (b) G one octave. 2nd finger changes its position
across the strings.

    (c) A one octave. 3rd finger changes its position
across the strings.

    'Broken', and then together as in Stage VII.

B. *Bowing*

A three-string exercise with a more advanced theme can
be introduced. The progression of notes is still simple,
but the bowing movements will be more complicated.
The following exercise is for developing bow manipulation and cannot always be related to pieces.

Each group can be played once, twice, or four times
according to the requirements of the bowing. It is also
possible to start on middle string, the same notes in a
different order. This will prepare the way for pieces with
well-known bowing difficulties, e.g. Bach's Partita in E.
The bowing movement is from middle bow to upper half.

Examples of other bowings

C. *Theory and notation*

Having played minor scales, it is now easier to understand their design, relationship to major scales, and their key signatures. When dealing with finger exercises (see 3. Chromatic Scales (page 121)) the use of double sharps and flats can be explained.

Other notation develops from bowings introduced, and in copying bars of examples.

D. *Some other incentives*

Two suggestions:

    1. Unaccompanied, unconducted unison playing
    2. Accompaniment

1. For six or eight people to play a tune in unison with no help from piano or conductor is not easy, but with the right class it can give tremendous satisfaction, and the

training in listening and for ensemble playing is invaluable. Pupils can also learn to lead a group of players without counting beats beforehand.

It is best when tunes can be played from memory. Pupils can all have an opportunity to act as leader.

Folk tunes and dances are excellent material for this, but they are not the easiest things to play. Here are three which have proved most successful.[1]

[1] 'Galopede' is from *The Fiddler's Tune Book*, ed. P. Kennedy (O.U.P.). 'Old Mole' is from *The English Country Dance* Vol. IV and 'Wheatley Processional' from *Morris Tunes* Set VI, both collected by C. Sharp (Novello).

Wheatley Processional

2. *Accompaniment*

This kind of work is usually attempted by an orchestra or ensemble class, but it is useful now and then to introduce it to the violin class. A solo singer or instrumentalist can be accompanied by the violinists without a conductor. (The teacher may have to write MS arrangements for some pupils.) Violins playing three or four different parts are, however, seldom satisfactory. If a cellist is not available it may be necessary to hold the bass line on the piano. Song accompaniments can be arranged, and pupils can be trained to listen to the soloist, and even watch, and feel, the breathing and phrasing without any stick-waving. One violin class can accompany another. A class at Stage V can play a piece they have learnt, and a class at Stage VII or VIII can accompany it, playing in parts. This is a useful innovation at an instrumental concert.

15

STAGE IX

Position work

A. Playing in different positions without shifts, and preparing for shifts.

B. Reading in positions
C. Shifting and changes of position
} To run concurrently.

At this stage one hopes to find pupils taught in a violin class clamouring for individual lessons, but for a variety to reasons these are not always available, and an attempt of introduce position work to the class must be made.

The drills and exercises set out in this chapter are not based on any particular theory or method of violin playing, but they have proved useful in introducing position work to groups.

It has long been a tradition to start beginners in the first position, and later to introduce the third and fifth positions, and as a result the second and fourth have often been neglected. Experiments have been tried in which the pupil plays anywhere on the instrument from the start, his fingers playing in tune with each other and related to the open strings. I have not had the courage to do this with a beginner, but once made an attempt to start an adult class of beginners, none of whom had ever played the instrument earlier, in the third position. The experiment was reasonably successful, but very little suitable printed music was available, and results did not really justify the enormous amount of manu-script-writing which was necessary. I do, however, attempt to get away from the traditional static approach of first–third–fifth positions and substitute the idea that a free movement of the hand is essential for playing in all positions. There is no real reason why playing in the higher positions should be more difficult than in the first.

A.

1. *Explain the three main reasons for playing in different positions.*

    (a) Higher notes can be reached.

    (b) Passage work is easier: e.g.

    (c) Tone quality can be more varied by the use of the colour of different strings.

It is to be hoped that by this time pupils will have a well-poised violin hold: strong but not stiff.

(d) Explain the numbering of positions. Up to now, only the first position has been used. Place the 1st finger on the usual 2nd finger sound, whether ♯, ♮, or ♭; this is the second position. Place the 1st finger on the usual 3rd finger sound, whether ♯, ♮, or ♭; this is the third position. Place the 1st finger on the usual 4th finger sound, whether ♯, ♮, ♭; this is the fourth position. It is useless to go further in this way, for we have no more than four fingers, so return to the open string and ally finger and letter name of note, e.g.:

On A string

1st finger on B, ♯, ♮, ♭, first position
  ,,   ,,   ,,   C, ,, ,, ,, second position
  ,,   ,,   ,,   D, ,, ,, ,, third position
  ,,   ,,   ,,   E, ,, ,, ,, fourth position
  ,,   ,,   ,,   F, ,, ,, ,, fifth position
  ,,   ,,   ,,   G, ,, ,, ,, sixth position
  ,,   ,,   ,,   A, ,, ,, ,, seventh position

and further if you wish.

2. (a) Slide each finger in turn up and down any string at harmonic pressure, falling into place with greater weight at the top and bottom of the string. The 3rd finger is usually the best to begin with. Keep the glissando movement as free as possible and see that the thumb does not get stuck round the base of the neck. Encourage the sensation of getting over the top of the strings, not creeping up from underneath.

(b) It will help sometimes to get a relaxed movement if the left elbow is held by the right hand, or placed on a table or ledge.

3. Both pizz. and arco.

(a) Place first finger on any note on G, D, or A string. Give this by ear. 'Put your finger on the D string on this sound.' Do not place it very high at first—up to fifth position is usually safe.

(b) Play 1st finger scale. Pattern III. One octave. Pupils will find that fingers have to be placed closer together and that more weight of finger is required.

(c) 1st finger scales starting on different strings in different places. One octave.

4. Tunes by ear, within the octave. They can be the same tunes that were used in earlier stages for new finger patterns, e.g. nursery rhyme tunes; Bells of Vendome; Duke Street; Drink to Me Only.

B. *Reading in Positions*

1. Tunes that have been played by ear, written on the blackboard with appropriate fingering. Some manuscript may be needed here also.
   Simple notation.

2. Tunes or studies of which pupils are unlikely to know the sound. At present it is not easy to find suitable published music for this stage in any position but the third.

   This is the moment when pupils have to learn to read notation all over again, and they will find it very disconcerting. 1st fingers play 3rd finger notes and vice-versa; open strings come in the wrong places, but if pupils have been encouraged to think and read in intervals in all previous stages, the difficulties are not so great.

   While these attempts at reading are being made, introduce:

C. *Shifting and changes of positions*

   Musically, most players would avoid a shift from one position to another on the same finger, but the following exercises 1(a)–(f) have been useful. Not only will they introduce a sensation of flexible movement, but they will also develop a habit of a guiding finger.

1. Shifting from one position to another on the same finger. The finger weight is released for the slide, but remains on the string.

   (a) Scales of one octave on one string played with one finger.

(b) Interval jumps on one string with one finger. Play **very** slowly.

It is a good plan to play both (a) and (b) with a crotchet silence between every note. Place the finger first, then imagine the sound of the note to come during the silence and then play that sound either pizzicato or arco.

(c) Repetition of exercise (b) with decoration:

(d) Repeat again changing rhythm or bowing

(e) After practising these exercises for a time arrange the bowing so that the shift down does not always coincide with the change of bow.

All these exercises should be carried out by different fingers on each string, starting on a suitable key-note, and always on one string. To do this with the 3rd and 4th is not easy.

(f) Interval leaps using different fingers but the shift always made on the same finger. Crossing strings.

All these exercises should also start in other positions than the 'first'.

2. *Moving positions from one finger to another*

   (a) The accepted rule is that the finger last used shall move into the new position (whether moving up or down), the new finger only falling into position when the new position has been reached.

Examples of this are to be found in nearly every violin exercise or study book:

The intermediary note in brackets to be sounded at first, but gradually not heard.

Then shorten the shifting note.

This type of exercise, the traditional first to third shift, is essential, but so often it is the only one introduced to beginners in position work. Other shifts equally important can be attempted in the early stages and may be based on scales on all four strings.

The examples below can be learned by ear or written in MS.

The suggestion that it is possible to step or stretch from one place to another will often develop a flexible movement and avoid stiff jerks. Just as a dancer will anticipate the first step, or someone about to jump will flex the knees, so the hand must be ready to move.

The following examples are written on A but should be played on all strings in all keys.

1. 1st to 2nd fingers. Different interval shifts

The logical downward shift of this exercise as in a mirror would be

with the constant note at the beginning of the bar.
Usually, however, pupils grasp the following sequence more easily, in spite of the difficulty of hitting the higher note in a different position; but the shifts are different in form and the pattern is not very logical.

2. 1st to 2nd fingers. Same interval shifts

3. 2nd to 3rd finger. Different interval shifts

and alternative downward
pattern as in (1)

4. 2nd to 3rd fingers. Same interval shifts.

5. 1st to 3rd fingers. Different interval shifts

and alternative downward
pattern as in (1)

6. 1st to 3rd fingers. Same interval shifts

7. Then the shifting fingers are changed within the same
exercise, for example:

(b) *Exceptions to rule* laid down in (2) (a)
When teaching the violin one of the many exceptions

to the rule is encountered at a very early stage. In one of the most usual scale shifts the rule cannot apply:

When moving to a higher position from a higher finger to a lower, move the new finger from the old position to the new, almost pushing the old finger out of the way. Shift on a semitone when possible.

    (a) An example of an exception based on arpeggio:

    (b) Another exercise.

3. *Transplanting exercises*
    (a) A note of constant pitch played with different fingers, and consequently in different positions. Exercises for this will be found in many violin study books. Example:

Repeat without rests, and in one bow.
    (b) Transplanting on a scale.

4. *Shifting on Scales*
(a)

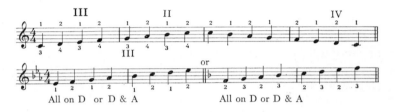

All on D or D & A   All on D or D & A

(b) Repeat with dotted rhythms.

5. Two octave, and some of the 'lower' three octave scales and arpeggios (as set in the syllabus of national examinations) will present less difficulty if the exercises given above have been practised in the necessary rhythms and bowings.

Studies and exercises from the usual violin repertoire may be used, but these are often more suited to the advanced music student.

There is no need to cover all this technical ground before introducing position work to the pupils. It is possible to find pieces in which whole phrases can be played in a position higher than that required for the piece as a whole. A useful example is the Purcell-(Clarke) Trumpet Voluntary, in which the first eight bars are played in the third position (making the trill and turn possible) followed by the next eight bars in the first position.

Pupils are often intrigued by the 'new high notes', and this is the moment to introduce one or two pieces which require a higher position on the E string. The keen players enjoy trying to play in the higher position and the lazy ones are obliged to follow suit because these notes are not to be found anywhere else on the violin!

Besides the graded pieces for teaching issued by many music publishers it is often possible to introduce pupils at this stage to a real violin sonata. Those most suitable for class work are:

     Corelli   No 8 in E Minor
        ,,   No. 9 in A
     Handel   Sonata in F

It is rare to be able to attempt works more difficult than these in class, but on three occasions I have found it possible to present the following:

     Vivaldi Concerto   A Minor
     Bach Double Concerto
     Mozart Concerto in D
        ,,   ,,   ,, G

An attempt too was made to play pieces lighter in texture, some of the easier Kreisler pieces for instance, and once we had quite a flashy performance of Monti's Czardas, my contention being that light music is often more difficult to play well, with good taste, than the accepted classics.

The children who formed these classes (approximately six in each) started at the age of eight in a Primary School. After being transferred to Secondary and Grammar Schools, the children continued in the same violin class, returning after school hours to the Primary School for lessons.

The works in the list above were performed before the class was divided, when its members reached the age of fourteen, into groups of three for a year. After this, private lessons were arranged.

The division into small groups was made to enable the children to enter for Grade VII Associated Board Examinations. It was not possible to deal with the theory, ear tests, and scales required for this Grade in classes of greater numbers. The children were of unusually even ability, and the encouragement and help given by their parents was enormous. It is not often one finds the ability, the will to work, and conditions which together make it possible to produce work of this kind in class.

16

THE VIOLA CLASS

Though this book is concerned almost wholly with the teaching of the violin in class, it may be helpful to insert a short chapter on the viola. The deep rich tone and many attractive qualities of this instrument are becoming recognized more and more and an increasing number of players in classes and orchestras change over to it, while others choose it in the first instance.

Whenever possible pupils should be taught by a viola player, for there is no getting away from the fact that the viola has a different voice and presents problems differing from those of the violin.

When a viola player is not available, the violin teacher must do his best, and it is said on good authority that in the earliest stages the same basic principles apply to both instruments.

A. *Beginners on the viola*
    1. Beginners on the viola can be taught in class in exactly the same way as beginners on the violin. The same holds and manipulative exercises can be introduced, but the *written* music should be in the alto clef, and there is no difficulty in reading notation if it is introduced in the same way as in the violin class.

2. If pupils are small, violins can be strung *with viola strings*. Young children can play even on half or three-quarter sized violins strung in this manner.

3. Pupils in Secondary or Grammar schools, and members of adult classes, should have a real viola if possible or they will feel resentful at being fobbed off with a makeshift instrument.

B. *Players changing from violin to viola*

1. In my scheme this usually occurs about Stage VI. Simple pieces written in the alto clef are given straight away and much reading is done. As a rule players do not take long to get used to the new clef.

2. After this preliminary stage, work can be resumed at Stage V but all a fifth lower—back one stage to consolidate work done in the violin class, in order to make pupils feel more at home on the new instrument.

   After a year, it is more than ever desirable to find a viola player to teach the class. If this proves impossible the teacher must continue on violin class lines, but viola players taught by violinists can generally be detected!

3. It is generally thought that a viola player must have a long arm and a large hand and, if started with the violin, the ability to produce a good full tone. This is a mistaken idea, for some very small people play the viola extremely well. Pupils of mine who have played with a fluffy tone on the violin and were always on top of their strings 'because they disliked squeaks', have turned out to be excellent viola players, because they had to press harder on the instrument in order to produce any sound at all. So the only qualification really necessary is a wish to play the instrument!

The size of violas can differ enormously. The most satisfactory size for school use appears to be about 15½–16 inches. If anything smaller is needed a large violin can be used.

Enormous care must be taken to make the hold, chin rest, and pad quite comfortable, otherwise the use of a larger, heavier, instrument may produce bad posture. Sometimes it is necessary to organize a 'mixed' class of violin and viola players, but it is not easy to run a class of this kind for any length of time.

Repertoire has been limited in the past, but is improving rapidly. Even so, much MS may be needed. There are many adaptations of violin music for the viola, but it is extraordinarily difficult to find any which make use of the C string; a sad omission, for that string reveals one of the essential characteristics of the viola. It is sometimes possible to use cello music for beginners on the viola.

When adapting violin music the part should be transposed down a fifth and the piano part rearranged. To attempt to play at the same pitch with an occasional drop of the octave is always awkward and often unmusical.

EARLY STAGES OF ORCHESTRA AND ENSEMBLE GROUPS

One of the main reasons for learning to play an instrument is to be able to play with others, and playing in a large group can be a great incentive to work. Care must be taken, however, that the violin class is not regarded as an orchestra or ensemble group, for this class is best considered as the equivalent of the traditional individual lesson in which pupils learn to play their instrument. Nevertheless, when building up a string class (especially in a school which has no established orchestra), keep future possibilities in mind and encourage a fair proportion of players to learn the violin, viola, and cello. Just as one hopes that individual pupils, when sufficiently advanced, will have opportunities for part playing and becoming members of an orchestra, so should class-taught pupils have similar opportunities apart from the weekly lesson.

Conditions are seldom favourable for this, and in order to create them much planning and organizing may be necessary.

Players of wind instruments usually pass through the elementary stages more quickly than those learning stringed instruments, and if classes of both kinds are started at the same time it is wiser to keep the groups separate for a little while. Not only is technique so different, but the difficulty of finding simple music in keys which suit both strings and wind is so great that players and conductors are apt to feel frustrated and depressed. Even at more advanced stages, constant arrangements and adaptations will be necessary.

Whenever possible the orchestra should be coached or conducted by someone who plays an orchestral instrument, for much time can be saved and better results achieved if the teacher can *show* what is wanted, instead of merely talking about it.

The orchestra (with several players to a part) is likely to emerge earlier from the string class than ensemble groups (each player holding an individual part), because many schools are so keen to have an orchestra to play at school concerts or at morning assembly. It is difficult to persuade enthusiasts that it would be better to wait until the string class is more advanced, and the teacher, often against his better judgement, finds it impossible to resist the demand.

Here are a few suggestions for the organization of an elementary orchestra, whether it consists of young children, older children, or adults.

Try to arrange for orchestra practice to be held apart from the violin class lesson, but if this is impossible the period allowed for the class can be divided into two parts, the earlier for the class itself, the later for orchestra practice. This is easy to arrange in Evening Institutes and similar organizations, but in schools where the lesson period is limited to forty or forty-five minutes it is not practicable. In these circumstances it is best to devote a whole lesson out of every three or four to the orchestra. It is usual, however, to have the orchestra out of school hours, unless of course the 4 p.m. school bus in rural areas makes this impossible.

If instrumental work has not been going for long and there is no established school orchestra for pupils in the violin class to join on special occasions, the orchestra can well be a glorified violin class, with pupils playing in two or three parts with piano. To make it more imposing it is always possible to introduce one or two percussion instruments, and perhaps a few very carefully chosen recorder players.

It is of course hoped that viola and cello classes will have started soon after the violin classes, so that the orchestra can be given a proper basis. Find out whether others in the school, children or members of staff, can play an instrument and persuade them to help the newly-formed orchestra. One of the first to be invited to play, or learn to play, an orchestral instrument, should be the master or mistress in charge of games and physical training; for times arranged for games and orchestra often clash, and however keen your musicians may be, there is always the problem of divided loyalties. So often too the physical education expert, with the training and understanding of the co-ordination of mind and muscle, turns out to be an extremely able player. Sometimes it is even possible to persuade the school caretaker to take part. This can solve many difficulties.

It is a tremendous incentive to the younger players to have members of the staff playing with them, particularly a headmaster who will tackle a double bass!

Before the orchestral rehearsal

There is often no opportunity for choice of room for rehearsal—it is usually the hall. Space is needed not only for playing but for instrument cases, and the hall is often best unless it is very large.

Lighting is important. If there are big windows, arrange the players with their backs to the light; it is impossible to see a conductor against the glare of windows.

1. Arrange stands, chairs, music, and percussion instruments if used. This is the responsibility of the teacher in the first place, but others should be trained to do this work as soon

as possible. If the hall is narrow, it is best to disregard the platform. A wide curve seating is more satisfactory than a deep elongated curve. This can be arranged if the conductor stands at the side of the hall. A is preferable to B.

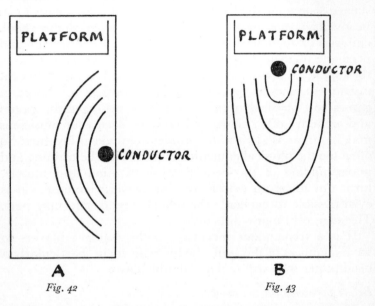

A

Fig. 42

B

Fig. 43

The relative position of the sections of the orchestra is a matter of personal preference.

2. Plan the seating so that not all the better players are in front. It is easier to play in the front of the orchestra than at the back. First and second violins should be equally divided according to ability, and it is often an advantage to have an able player with an elementary one at each desk. If there is need for a group of beginners who cannot yet attempt first and second violin parts, place them right in the middle of the orchestra where they can hear sounds

all round them. If they are on the fringe of the group they become more and more timid.

3. All parts should be lettered and bowed before being placed on the stands. Everyone knows there should never be more than two players to a stand; yet how often has one been obliged to allow three to crowd at a stand because music has been lost or left at home. However long-sighted a player may claim to be, the evils of three to a stand are great. No one can sit in the correct position with relation to the stand; spines and necks get twisted, and bowing becomes cramped and crooked.

4. There should be folders for every desk marked Vln. I Desk I, Vln. I Desk II, etc. and players should be trained to make sure no loose bits and pieces of music are inside anything else, and to close the folder at the end of every rehearsal.

5. In setting the time for a rehearsal always allow ten or fifteen minutes for unpacking and tuning, and have a zero hour for the start of actual playing (e.g. 4 p.m. rehearsal. Begin playing 4.15 p.m.)

6. Chairs should be wooden kitchen chairs. Canvas or curved plastic chairs are fatal to posture and comfort.

7. Players must be taught how to sit.
   With children it is best to insist that they sit on the edge of the chair with both feet on the ground, as though about to sprint. If legs are short it may be necessary to place a wooden violin case or box on the floor on which to rest the feet and make the young player comfortable. With older children who may have very long legs there are other difficulties for violin and viola players. The right knee must be got out of the way somehow.
   With older people rehearsals generally last longer, and players will feel the need of support in the back, but on the whole, leaning back is not a good plan, and crossing

the legs when playing is one of those things which are just not done.

8. The angles between seat, stand, and conductor's baton are important. It should be possible to see both the music and the stick without turning the head or looking up from the music. I am often a little worried when I hear a conductor say 'I shall not begin until I can see every eye.'

And if two players do not sit at the correct angle with the stand they are liable to poke one another in the eye or ear with their bows. The violins of both players should point to the top left hand corner of their music and then there will be no trouble.

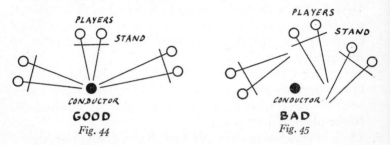

GOOD
Fig. 44

BAD
Fig. 45

String players need room to bow freely; cellists need an incredible amount of space. Wind players can do with far less, but avoid two flautists to one stand and leave room for trombones.

9. Never fear that careful tuning is a waste of time. It is of the utmost importance. The teacher may have to do a considerable amount of this tuning, but at least a tuning drill can be attempted.

It is wise to have a general tuning first. Instruments are not always in first-class condition and pupils are apt to drop their violins in their cases on the way to school. Pegs will have moved and strings may be loose; wind players need to warm up their instruments.

Careful tuning of the strings to A at the beginning of the rehearsal goes for nothing if later on the D string is found to have slipped. And how difficult it is to persuade people to attempt to tune quietly!

After the general tuning has been done, more detailed and careful tuning should follow; each department of the orchestra being checked individually, and even single strings, especially the lower ones. The indispensable double bass player must be given a chance to hear his strings; they are particularly difficult to hear when other people are making noises. Section leaders can be trained to help with tuning, and the seating of more advanced players with less able ones can also be a great help.

The rehearsal

It is rarely possible to carry out all one's intentions at an orchestra practice, however carefully rehearsals are planned and timed, but it may be helpful to bear the following points in mind:

1. Allow the orchestra to play itself in.

   Try to keep things going even if the pupils get lost. Don't stop and make corrections after the first few bars, but let the players warm up.

2. After playing in, name *one* correction only. Rehearse it and play it, and then go on to the next item.

   Try not to give a long list of mistakes. For example—'At letter C there are two Fs; the B♭ four bars before F is out of tune; attack the chord three bars before E—' etc. People just don't remember.

3. An occasional rest is necessary, but do not keep any section of the orchestra inactive for long. This is particularly the case with children, who want to be 'doing' most of the time. One hopes they will learn something from listening to others being rehearsed but the idea that 'This

does not concern me' is apt to creep in. When rehearsing one section the others can be occupied with silent note learning.

4. Alternate between conducting and playing with the orchestra, and encourage the idea that listening is quite as important as looking at a conductor and playing.

5. Note learning must often be done during rehearsal. Playing in an orchestra is wonderful training for reading music, but most pupils will need help in this direction.

6. Although the conductor will have studied the score thoroughly and decided what is required musically, it is generally necessary to rehearse technical points with an elementary orchestra if musical playing is to result. It is useless to ask for a *pp* or a *ff* or to make a phrase sound as it should if the players have not the technical skill to produce these musical effects.

Intonation, attack, changes of tempo, gradation of tone, starts and last notes, dynamics and stick-following are all technical in the first place and must be practised if possible by extracting material from the pieces being studied, or by devising exercises on scales, chords or cadences.

7. Even in the most elementary string orchestras it is possible to grade the amount of tone. Beginners are often timid in their movements and the first aim should be good solid forte playing with as much freedom of bow movement as possible. But if this is allowed to go on too long pupils may form the habit of sawing away at a good *mf* all the time. Most people after the very early lessons can play loudly; playing softly is often tiring and frustrating, and much harder to accomplish.

There are of course other points to be considered, but the seven mentioned above may be regarded as the most essential.

Rehearsing of sections of the orchestra

The quality of playing in an orchestra may improve enormously if opportunities are made for sectional rehearsals. The ideal arrangement for a fair-sized orchestra is for each section to be coached individually in part of the rehearsal time—first violins, second violins, violas, etc., all separately, but time is usually limited and there are seldom enough coaches to allow of such a plan. When there is only one teacher, or the orchestra is very small, the best that can be done is to devote part of each weekly rehearsal to the coaching of one section of players. Arrange a rota, say, first week full orchestra, second week strings, third week wind, fourth full orchestra again, with more full rehearsals towards the end of a term.

Help given in this way will probably consist of note-learning, fingering, bowing, and blowing, and the players will gain confidence. This kind of plan is usually found to be a saving of rehearsal time in the end.

Choice of music

This is the most important and difficult work in dealing with elementary orchestras. Whenever possible find music in which the parts are of equal interest to all instruments— but the members of a newly-formed orchestra may be found to consist, say, of two violins and a cello able to play at approximately the standard of Grades V and VI (Associated Board), and the rest may be very limited in technique and key. In this case the elementary players are sometimes happier for a little while with a dull part, but a great effort must be made to introduce a piece with a tune for the second violins or violas.

If the group consists of players of varying ability, choose music for those of the intermediate stage. Adapt and arrange parts requiring agility for the more advanced pupils and simplify them for the most elementary. This takes an enormous amount of time, but if the music is good, the results are certainly worth the effort. Always choose a work that has a full score; if there is only a piano-conductor and the music is good it is worth while writing out your own full score.

Remember that slow pieces often need vibrato to make them sound right. A quick rhythmic piece or a tune that moves along is often more satisfactory, even if the notes look more difficult on paper.

It is difficult to know how far to stretch the powers of young players or adult amateurs in an orchestra. We have been brought up on the principle that it is better to play an easy piece well than a difficult piece badly. And yet after the early stages have been passed through the players need something to get their teeth into. Then it may be great fun and very stimulating to have a bash at overtures and symphonies which are really far too difficult for an orchestra in an early stage; but not too early, or the result may be farcical. And remember that this kind of performance is best carried out in private and not before an audience. Ears become deaf when people are struggling with difficult notes and the sounds produced are often unfortunate—to say the least. If playing is to become progressively more advanced we must often present our pupils with music which cannot be played at sight. That is why it is so important to coach and teach an elementary orchestra and not only conduct it.

Most children and amateur adults want to improve their playing and do not mind being worked hard, provided they know the reason for making an effort. I believe it is a fallacy to imagine they must want to play things through. If they work well and produce good results they will experience the feeling of satisfaction and determination one hopes to achieve at the end of every rehearsal.

Part playing, chamber music and ensemble groups

The first introduction to part playing is likely to be attempted in the instrumental class.

The obvious beginning, with instruments at the same pitch, is:

1. A scale in canon.
2. A simple round.
3. A progression of simple chords against which the teacher or a more advanced pupil can play a tune.
   (See Chapter 12, page 113. Other incentives 1b.)
4. Published duets, trios, and quartets for players of some ability of which there are now a number for violins or cellos—few alas for viola.
5. Published works—mostly trios for violins—for combined classes of differing ability. One part open strings only, second violin simpler than first.
6. This part-playing to be done sometimes with piano, sometimes without.

The term Chamber Music or Ensemble Group has always implied to me one player to a part, although technically this is not, of course, correct. It is quite amazing how playing will improve if pupils will make the attempt to play in such a group.

If four young players are introduced to quartet playing, their interest is usually held for life.

The real string quartet is the most satisfying combination and there is no need for the players to be able to play the notes of a classical work to experience this kind of music: much simple material can be used. If one is not lucky enough to have the necessary players of the right ability on the right instrument for a true quartet, music can be found for other combinations: say two violins and cello, three violins and cello, and a pianist can also be encouraged to join. It is not easy, however, to find elementary works for the string trio, or strings and wind groups. Whatever the combination, the most important point is that each player holds an individual part while playing with others.

To begin with it is wise to choose a straightforward diatonic work such as an arrangement of a hymn tune or folk-song. These being familiar, the players can keep their place and realize more easily whether they are right or wrong.

The quartet can then move on to individual movements from some of the less well-known works of the seventeenth and eighteenth centuries (some early works of Haydn and Mozart are most useful), or they can attempt some of the recently published music written with the elementary player in view. Some of these are modern in idiom without the difficult notes of most modern works. They are usually greatly enjoyed by young players, and accepted by them in their own right and as an introduction to the classical quartets.

In the search for suitable chamber music for elementary players one naturally turns to some of the earlier instrumental music, say of Purcell and his contemporaries and predecessors, but beware their apparently easy notes. They are often a snare as they are extremely difficult rhythmically and musically, and because of their vocal texture are not always satisfying to the inexperienced string player.

18

ADJUDICATIONS, EXAMINATIONS, FESTIVALS, CONCERTS

Even the most enthusiastic players need an occasional incentive, a definite goal towards which to work; and examinations and adjudications at festivals may be essential at one stage or another—although my personal preference is for playing festivals and concerts.

Many organizations now cater for class-taught pupils. Young instrumentalists have plenty of opportunities to play with others, or have their work criticized by an understanding adjudicator, but this was not so when I began class-teaching.

Syllabuses of the early grades of the national examination did not fit the plan of finger patterns which was developing in my experimental classes, and the keys of pieces and the scales set for examination were not suited to it either, so for a short time I planned a syllabus based on the stages of work done in class, and invited a string player to adjudicate.

To make the examination more of an event it was not held at the school but at my own home. The children played as individuals and not as a class. Those taking part were expected to listen to others in their class and could stay longer if they wished.

The grades in the syllabus were based on the stages given in earlier chapters of this book. Children could choose any pieces learned in class during the previous four months, but the choice was guided. They were easily persuaded to choose contrasting pieces, and a more difficult piece was expected to follow one really too easy for the grades. This method prevented general work in class from being held up by learning set pieces, and the adjudicator heard a greater variety of music, though his task may have been more difficult. Only once or twice were marks awarded; it was usual to have comments and suggestions by the adjudicator after the playing of each child.

Here are a few examples of syllabuses for the earliest grades.

Grade I. (Stages I and II in plan of class-work)
1. Scales G. D. A. One octave, separate bows.
2. Open-string bowing exercise.
3. Exercise for left-hand finger-placing, pizzicato, on one string.
4. Piece. Bow and fingers together.
5. Playing at sight. Open strings, pizzicato $\wp$ and $\wp$ only.

Grade II (Stage III in plan of class work)
1. Scales G. D. A. One octave, separate and slurred.
2. Open-string bowing exercises.
3. Exercises for left-hand finger placing, pizzicato, crossing any strings.
4. Piece (arco) Pattern I.
5. Sight-reading using left-hand fingers, pizzicato, or open strings (arco) $\circ$ ' $\wp \cdot$ ' $\wp$ ' $\wp$ ' $\sqcup$

Grade III (Stage IV in plan of class work)
1. Scales G. D. A.   One octave, separate, slur two or four.
      „   C. G.   One octave, separate, starting 3rd finger.
2. Exercise or study from class book.
3. Piece in Pattern I or Pattern II.

4. Sight-reading. o − i − ♮3 fingering only.
5. Simple ear tests.

Grade IV (Stage V in plan of class work)
1. Scales as in Grade III and G in two octaves, separate and slur two and four.
2. Exercise or study.
3. Piece. Patterns I and II.
4. Sight-reading.
5. Ear tests.

There were twelve grades in all. A slow pupil could plod through all quite happily, whereas a quicker one would jump some grades. The length of time a pupil had been learning was always given and taken into account.

Grades VIII and IX were approximately equal to the standard of the Associated Board Grade II.

Here is an example of a later grade related to Associated Board Grade III.

Grade XI
1. Scales (a) Major G. A. B. Two octaves, separate, and slur eight to bow.
                 B. C. D. Two octaves, separate.
      (b) Minor (harmonic) G. A. B. Two octaves, separate, and slur eight to bow.
                 C. D. Two octaves, separate.
Arpeggios.
      (a) Major G. A. B. Two octaves, slur three
                B. C. D. Two octaves separate bows
      (b) Minor G. A. B. Two octaves slur three
                C. D.   Two octaves separate bows
2. Study.
3. Piece.
4. Sight-reading.
5. Ear tests.

These later grades were seldom used, however, except for tests, for it was better at this stage for pupils to enter for the Associated Board Examinations.

My great concern was to keep the standard of playing high, and because I believed that class-teaching, although it took a little longer, could produce technical and musical results equal to those achieved by individual teaching, I advised pupils to enter for an examination *a grade lower* than the one in which they were actually working. This meant they were examined on work which was well within their technical capacity and more attention could be given to musical effects. The results were usually very satisfactory, both for the children and their parents.

It is difficult to say how often it is wise to hold examinations or adjudications. So much depends on local conditions and the timing of other functions in the school and neighbourhood.

In my own case the most suitable time was the middle of the summer term, as it did not clash with the concert or playing festival given each year at Christmas. This became one of the traditional events at the school. Nevertheless, if I could provide sufficient incentives by means of playing with others or preparing for solo or group performances, I would prefer to do without adjudications and would never encourage them in the early stages.

Less time is wasted and the results seem better.

The playing festival

Festivals for instrumentalists to come together and play are becoming more and more popular both with school children and older players. Various kinds are now organized, some lasting a day only, others a week-end, or several days at a holiday course. These can be of great value if planned with care and well prepared beforehand. Those taking part have a far greater opportunity to play than at an adjudication or a competitive festival.

At combined school festivals it is often satisfactory to have graded music, so that all players take part in beginners' items, and as the pieces become more difficult all except the more advanced pupils drop out.

Choice of music is a matter of first importance, and music organizers and string teachers are becoming experienced in choosing the right kind of material, but almost always there are too many items in the programme.

It must be remembered that for most young players it is an exciting experience to come from an isolated violin class and play with a crowd of others. The sounds are disconcerting, and the children need time to know what is expected of them in new surroundings and with a teacher or conductor they have never met before.

It is the playing and rehearsing that are so important and there is rarely time allowed for a thorough rehearsal. The length of the concert does not matter: it can always be lengthened by a performance by a solo artist.

For half an hour of actual playing time at the Festival Concert, allow an extra half-hour for tuning, and three hours of rehearsal at least (with breaks of course).

The administrative side of these festivals is of enormous importance, and I am always full of admiration for the devoted people who take on this work. So much of the success of the rehearsal and concert depends on organization: provision of cloak-rooms, instrumental rooms, food, arrangement of stands (particularly if the performers have to bring stands with them and the hall or room cannot be set out beforehand), and seating. Players must sit as an orchestra and not stand to play on these occasions. There are timetable arrangements to be made, and notices of music to be bought, learned and played by each class taking part.

One is always grateful when string teachers find time to come with their pupils, for not only do they look after their charges and help with the perpetual problems of tuning, broken strings and bridges, etc. but they sit in the orchestra and play with everyone else. This gives the children a feeling of security and encourages them to play better. It also helps to make the festival the right kind of social event.

Competitive festivals

As stated before, my own preference has always been for playing festivals, but if pupils in a class have wished to enter for a competition, they have done so on their own responsibility, with a few minutes' individual help at odd times when it has been possible to fit in a short lesson.

The school concert

The school concert offers the main opportunity for instrumentalists to perform, and when a tradition for such a function has been established, it is possible to plan a well-balanced concert of singing and playing.

When instrumental work is in its early stages it is difficult to do the class justice. It is possible to find music of first-class quality for very young singers, but for instrumentalists, especially string players, it is most difficult to find music of the same merit. If a string class or group is to perform in a mixed concert, great care must be taken to place it in the programme where it will not sound insignificant. Added to this, time is needed for arranging chairs and stands (if music is used), and for tuning.

After an interval is therefore a good moment.

In the earliest stages of class work, open-string pieces with exciting piano parts can sound quite imposing. Later on, when the problems of finger-placing arise, a class may not sound very good to the uninitiated listener, so do your best to prevent the string class from following the school choir or a brass band.

It is indeed better to arrange for strings to have a small concert of their own until they are a little more advanced. This can take the form of a demonstration. 'How we have learned to play the violin in class.' It will serve as revision for pupils and will show their parents what is being taught in the lessons. Half an hour or forty minutes goes by quickly in a bird's-eye view demonstration, gradually building up from the very earliest stages to the latest.

After this, a solo item, not by a child in the class, but by the best artist one can get or afford (preferably a string player). Finally, some more combined playing, either three or four carefully rehearsed pieces, or even better, the class playing one or two songs in which the audience can join. The whole programme should never exceed one hour.

When planning concerts after this very early stage, the main problem has been to keep the programme short and yet give everyone a chance of playing as much as possible. As classes grow in number and work progresses, the possibilities are great and items for a concert can be chosen from pieces being learned in the class-rooms, or special combined items can be arranged.

At the Junior School at which I taught for ten years, an annual concert for instrumentalists only was held. Occasionally singers were invited to join the players, but the violin classes were the first consideration. Some parents and teachers became interested enough to have violin, viola, and cello lessons, either in class or individually, and as time went on a rather unbalanced string orchestra came into being. The first performance consisted of a demonstration of class work of the kind already outlined. After this, as numbers increased and playing became more advanced the following kinds of items were introduced into programmes:

1. *Violin classes*

    (a) Beginners' pieces. All violinists taking part.
    (b) Individual class performance.
    (c) Special arrangements.
        (i) Children's own compositions.
        (ii) Medley of nursery rhymes, chosen by children, linked and arranged by an interested parent, with parts for those of different ability.
    (d) Violin duets, trios and quartets.
    (e) Folk dances. Unison playing, unaccompanied, unconducted.
    (f) Accompaniment (piano also) of a singer, unconducted.
    (g) Accompaniment (piano also) of another violin class.
    (h) Class playing of movements from such works as Corelli and Handel sonatas, Mozart concerto, Bach Double Concerto.

2. As viola and cello classes became advanced enough to join in:

    (a) Orchestral items. Polychordia Albums. Later on. Movements from Bach Suite in D, Handel, Avison, and once or twice something of a different style attempted, such as The Skaters' Waltz or Mock Morris.
    (b) Carol festivals—Accompaniments.
    (c) String quartets. (Sometimes family quartets.)

3. Ex-pupils of the school who had become Junior Exhibitioners at the R.C.M. and R.A.M. returned to take part in some concerts, both as soloists and to help the younger players.

4. Some children left the school, but returned for violin lessons as there were no facilities for lessons at their new schools.

In dealing with so many young instrumentalists the planning of rehearsals was important, but far from easy. It was necessary to show children how to walk on to a platform, how to carry an instrument up steps without damage, and general platform manners. When planning a time-table of rehearsals one had to remember that children of seven and eight years of age had to be in bed by seven o'clock; that parents were not home from work until about that time; that children returning from other schools needed an evening meal and had homework to do. It was rare to get everyone together until the final rehearsal.

With about 150 players taking part there was not much room for an audience, but it did not seem to matter very much.

19

CONCLUSION

My intention is not to present a method or school of violin playing, but to set out a plan of work for teachers inexperienced in a group approach. No matter what method of violin playing is followed, or how experienced a teacher may be in teaching individuals, a class technique has to be acquired by most of us, or the work will not succeed.

Just occasionally one meets the teacher who is successful in class with individual methods, but this is very rare indeed. Usually this approach develops into a series of five-minute lessons for each pupil, while the others are unoccupied, and perhaps tiresome. I have even seen some classes in which children have been doing homework in other subjects, or reading 'comics'. This is *not* class work.

A class technique implies that everyone is simultaneously occupied with the business of learning to play the violin. The class must be taught as a whole nearly all the time, and this can be done without neglecting the needs of the individual.

When teaching one pupil at a time, it is usually possible to give him a sense of achievement at every stage: it is much more difficult to give every child in a violin class this same sense of achievement in every lesson. It should of course be our aim to make each child in the group feel that something has been accomplished at every stage, no matter how small in detail, but this is extremely difficult to do with pupils of uneven ability. Careful preparation is essential not only of stages and in the selection of material but—most important of all—the preparation of a plan of presentation. Every single item, whether musical or technical, should be presented in the most direct manner possible and in the simplest words, and it will sometimes help to rehearse explanations aloud. It is very difficult indeed to take nothing for granted, to teach one thing at a time and to be alert to the danger of muddled explanations. There are some people termed born teachers; people sensitive to the response of a class, who appear to teach by instinct and are able to turn some unexpected happening to good account, seemingly on the spur of the moment; but on looking more deeply into the matter we usually find that these talented teachers are the ones who have the clearest plan. Because they know exactly where they are going, the children know too. They have detailed plans for the current lesson and those immediately following, less detailed ones for a term or a year, and overall plans for the whole period during which a particular class is likely to function. Experiment and modification as the work progresses is essential, but a general plan there must be.

It is upon this plan that we build our teaching skills and class-room technique. In attempting to put a plan of class work on paper I am well aware that a written explanation of a technical skill is not really satisfactory. I am anxious too that no one should accept another's plan in its entirety. I would, however, urge anyone interested in class teaching to watch an experienced teacher at work; this will be of far more value than any books or lectures on the subject.

All of us who teach are concerned with the quality of our work. Naturally we all want our pupils to be good musicians and able violinists, but we cannot always find the right approach to achieve this in class.

Every teacher has a different sense of standard, according to temperament, background, training, taste, and sensitivity. We all differ greatly in our attitude and do not always have the opportunity to discover whether our work is of high quality or not. It is a frightening thought that high standards are our concern as teachers; standards are in ourselves, irrespective of the ability of our pupils. Neither is it always realized by young teachers that high standards are in no way related to the ability to play difficult music. The most elementary pieces can be played with the same quality of style and musicianship as a really advanced work; alternatively, there can be bad playing both at elementary and advanced levels. This statement may appear to be stupidly obvious to most, but I do so often find the words 'high standard' misused.

There seem to be two main approaches to violin class work and many of us are constantly torn between the two. They are perhaps best illustrated by two extreme examples.

The first was a Secondary Modern School for girls, where the teacher took two classes of ten children each. When I heard them they had been learning for two years. The style of every child was superb, the posture and movements of them all were lovely to see; easy and relaxed. Intonation was impeccable and no fault could be found in tone quality and phrasing. My admiration of the quality of the teaching and for the teacher was great, but it was a mystery to me how she had managed to hold their interest on the very elementary pieces they were able to play so well. Although they were enjoying their lesson, the ground they had covered in two years was very limited and I doubted whether they were developing the necessary self-sufficiency to encourage them to go on playing after they left school. I learned later that the girls seldom carried on. True, there was no youth or amateur orchestra to which they could belong, but perhaps this teacher had been too keen in never allowing a fault to pass or a bad habit to arise.

The second example was a Secondary Modern School for boys. There were over 150 boys learning string instruments, and almost before they knew how to hold them properly they were playing in an orchestra. Everyone was having a wonderful time, the stands were heavy with sheet music and all the boys were prepared to play anything put in front of them. Posture was frightful, intonation inches out, the noise indescribable—but the enthusiasm tremendous. How the teacher survived the week, let alone the term or year, I shall never know. The instrumental work was proving to be an answer to many problems, the school was in a tough district and the headmaster was loud in his praises of the work being done. The devoted teacher ran a youth orchestra for school leavers and many boys asked for private lessons, when unfortunately they often had to correct many bad habits and serious faults, and sometimes lost heart as a result.

It is impossible not to commend the work of both these teachers. Both had a strong and vivid personality and were devoted to the job; but surely these two aims or approaches might be compatible? Should it not be possible to play well *and* enjoy it? A balance of the two is the obvious solution, but how do we find that balance? It is particularly difficult for the young music student, about to embark on class teaching, to know when to be lenient and when to be firm; and sometimes a difficult situation will arise which an experienced teacher would avoid. Young teachers, anxious for pupils to play well, and determined that a class shall get at least one thing right, may come up against a group of small boys equally determined not to do as they are asked. Stalemate ensues, and eventually either the children take over the class and dictate to the teacher, or the class dwindles and the teacher decides that he can't teach or that the discipline of the school is bad or that violin class work is useless.

The experienced teacher will see the danger signal and be able to avoid this situation; he will know when to press a point home and when to give way without the class realizing it. To make a change because the class is getting restless or bored is not to take the line of least resistance; to alter the focus of concentration is no more than common sense. A return to the particular point can be made later, and there will be an adjustment of plans.

The inexperienced teacher will become sensitive to this as time goes on, but at first it is wise to plan for constant change and variety, and it is probably better to change too often than to get stuck on one thing. The lesson must be enjoyed and variety will help more than anything else in the early stages. It is so often a lack of understanding of this need for change and balance that brings about difficulties of class discipline, wastage, and low standards of playing.

It is also difficult to judge when something is good enough to leave. We all have different ideas and sometimes a piece has to be abandoned before it is as well played as we think it should be, but *remember* that it was abandoned and try returning to it in six months' time in the form of revision. The class will probably play it well and this will give the children a feeling of real achievement and progress.

On the whole I have found that people like to play well and to work hard if they are shown how. Occasionally, I know, one does meet players in amateur orchestras or chamber music groups who seem to resent help and whose pride is hurt if they are asked to work at music which seems easy; they prefer to play more difficult works, often beyond them, because it is grand to do so.

It is right that people should have the experience of playing great works and of getting to know them from the inside;
this is, in fact, one of the main reasons for encouraging them
to play at all. But it is sad if the playing never improves in
quality because the teacher imagines that interest will wane
if the players are asked to work and not just play. I am sure
this is not the case. Usually the best results are achieved if the
teacher can make the members of the group feel that he is
leading, coaching and training them, that he is part of the
group. Let him forget his conductor's stick occasionally; if
he can show the players what he wants instead of telling
them, it will help everyone. Players can be helped to make
the right kind of effort by the enthusiasm of the teacher, they
can be encouraged to seek help and are usually extremely
grateful for it. There are few things more rewarding to a
teacher than a response of effort from a group of children or
amateur musicians. Standards can then be high, no matter
what the ability of the group.

In the choice of music, it is obvious that we must try to
present works of all styles and periods, sometimes even works
that we ourselves dislike; although to teach something one
does not like oneself is seldom satisfactory. It does not come
off, and we would be wise to teach music that we ourselves
enjoy and feel to be worth while.

There is much lovely music of the seventeenth and
eighteenth centuries suitable to the technical ability of our
pupils, and this will always form the basis of our material.
Much as we should like to introduce our pupils to many
other kinds of music, its technical difficulty will sometimes
be too great. It is hard to find romantic, modern, or light
music that can be played to a reasonable standard in class,
or by amateur orchestras.

Works written specially for beginners on the violin are not

always musically worth while. Arrangements of songs or piano pieces of the nineteenth century are usually most unsatisfactory. Light music is often more difficult to play well than the accepted classics, and I have to admit that I have never succeeded in finding anything more modern than Bartók that can be played by elementary players in class or orchestras: and so we return again and again to the wealth of music of the seventeenth and eighteenth centuries.

Yet our search for music of other styles must go on, for everything should be offered to our pupils, and will be accepted by them. The limitations are technical and not a matter of taste or lack of enterprise. It is of course true that as teachers we often become conservative in our choice of music, and persist in teaching works which we believe to be good music and which we have found productive of good results. But we do sometimes misjudge the taste of our pupils and imagine that certain styles are acceptable and others not. Let us not assume that a light, tuneful waltz is likely to be more popular than a slow, solemn chorale—in fact a class given the choice between the two will usually choose the latter—or that a vigorous march will be more popular than a slow movement of Handel or Corelli. Children, particularly, are interested in a wide field of music ranging from Bach to Bartók if they are given the opportunity to play it, and it is up to us to ensure that, whatever the style of music— whether 'pop', light, old or new—it may be of the best quality and musically worth while.

The violin is a difficult instrument to play well; many begin in class and then drop it. Some teachers believe that it is wasteful to allow children to begin to learn such a difficult instrument unless they have ability. This ability can be assessed to a certain extent by tests, both musical and manipulative. A considerable amount of research has already been carried out on tests for musical aptitude, but there is still an enormous amount to be done on the manipulative side.

Teachers are gravely concerned by diminishing numbers in string classes, and serious thought must be given to preventing wastage. But what is wastage? Pupils give up for a great variety of reasons. The instrument may not be suited to them. Other interests may prove stronger. The teaching may be bad, or they may have little encouragement at home. But was it wasteful to have tried?

Tests of potential musical ability will help us to judge who may be most likely to do well, but there are always exceptions. I would much rather see everyone given a trial. A trial term, or even a trial year, can do no one any harm, and unless numbers are so great as to necessitate some means of weeding out, I would suggest that everyone should be given the opportunity to try. Some children who do not appear to have an ear for pitch or a sense of rhythm develop these faculties with the instrument in their hands.

Then too, there is welfare work. 'John can't seem to use his hands well; we thought the violin might help him'; or 'Jane doesn't seem to be any good at ordinary school subjects, but we do want to find something she *can* do'. Even if pupils learning for these reasons do not become able violinists and imaginative musicians, surely a year or so of co-ordinating hearing, touch, and sight cannot come amiss? Provided we are not neglecting a more talented child, can we really write these cases off as wastage?

In times past, long before violin classes were considered, many children started to play and left off, just as they do today; but if by any chance they began again in adult life it was noticeable that they had far greater ease and freedom of movement than those starting from the beginning. I have met a number of instances of this in Evening Institute classes,

Students tell me that they have never learned, but when they start to hold the violin and bow, it seems obvious they have handled them before. Further inquiry shows that they did have a few lessons at the age of seven or eight, but 'it was so long ago, I didn't think it would count'.

Many adults express the wish that they had been able to learn the violin, but explain that there was no opportunity. Nowadays nearly everyone has a chance to begin as a child. Should any of these leave off and start again as adults, they will find far less difficulty in learning.

The social side

Festive occasions for pupils learning to play an instrument can be of enormous value; indeed many teachers claim that much of their best work is done informally, away from regular weekly lessons.

Concerts, festivals, and examinations have already been mentioned as incentives, but there are others less formal and equally important. The ever-increasing number of summer schools for orchestral and chamber music players is indicative of the demand for this particular aspect of the work.

In speaking of the social side, however, I have in mind something that the average teacher can arrange without any very complicated organization: a small and informal musical party that does not require a large hall or the hiring of charabancs. A small group of people can meet together just to play, with no special function in view.

When I first arranged an afternoon of playing for my violin class pupils I did not realize the importance of this kind of event. I simply thought it would be fun to get my classes together, and to play. At the back of my mind I realized that after four terms some of the children should play in an orchestra of some kind, and I felt the need for closer contact with their parents. I had always encouraged parents to come and listen to their children's lessons, and had noticed that the progress of the children whose parents attended classes was most marked; so I invited children and parents to my own home (I am lucky to have a large sitting-room) for a musical party.

The success of this event may have been due partly to the fact that it was held in surroundings different from those of the weekly lessons, and chairs were more comfortable for the non-players than the ones in the average class-room. But I also believe that buns, tea, and lemonade were an added attraction.

Very easy music for violins and piano (no one played any other orchestral instrument at that time) was carefully chosen. I hoped that some of the parents could be encouraged to take part, but as they could not play the violin, I provided some toy percussion instruments. Some claimed that they could not read music, but were persuaded to do so for the first time. As the afternoon went on it was obvious that some greatly envied their children. They felt that this percussion business was not good enough and asked me if I would start a violin class for them. Of course I was delighted, but begged some of them to consider trying the viola or cello. At the end of the afternoon every instrument I possessed went out on loan to parents, and those to whom I had none to lend went off determined to find one.

In this way instrumental classes started for parents, and staff of the school. The Headmistress was a keen member of the group and this encouraged others to join; many more parents started to attend their children's lessons; one or two mothers who played the piano well made themselves responsible for accompanying classes and invited groups of children to their homes for supervised practice. This was one of the most useful results of the party, for as time went on I merely had to provide material and technical information, and the parents did the rest. They also took on much MS copying and some arranging. Family quartets were now a possibility, an orchestra was in sight, and informal musical evenings became an accepted event in many homes in the district.

I have to admit that today this kind of thing is more difficult to arrange, as there are so many counter-attractions; but even so, I still strive to achieve the same conditions that came about so naturally at my first school. This is still fairly easy to do in Primary Schools, but it is much more difficult to make contact with the parents of older children; not, I believe, because of any lack of interest on their part, but because the children tend to keep home and school apart in their minds, and the situation is different.

The Parent-Teachers Association in a school may form a useful link between the adults and music, but it usually leaves out the children. Even so, the Association can sometimes be persuaded to organize an evening of music as a social occasion, at which players of all ages are invited to take part.

Instrumental music is one of those activities in which people of all ages can share on equal terms. Grown-ups sometimes begin to learn to play an instrument to encourage their children, but will often find themselves enjoying it enormously for its own sake.

One of my most exciting experience as a class teacher was on the occasion of the Primary School concert already mentioned in the first chapter, when I suddenly realized that the 150 players whose ages ranged from seven to seventy would never have started to play an instrument had it not been for one small violin class. Most children played better than their parents, but age did not matter.

I became even more aware of this as I walked home from teaching on summer evenings and heard through open windows of practically every house I passed the sounds of string instruments; from one house the sound of a very simple piece played by a group of beginners, helped by the mother of one. Next door a Handel Sonata for two violins and further on, a real string quartet attempting Haydn or Mozart, or a solitary instrument practising a scale. Whole families, near neighbours, young and old, were all taking part; and this was the outcome of a simple, informal musical party.

Often I am asked by music teachers, keen to start instrumental work in their schools but not themselves violinists, whether they could have lessons and teach the children by keeping a few lessons ahead of them.

We all learn by imitation to a great degree; therefore the teacher must be able to hold his instrument well, draw a straight bow and produce a reasonable tone; and however simple the sounds or the piece played, it should be played in tune. This takes considerable time and effort and will depend on how much the teacher concerned is prepared to sacrifice in other ways. This plan has sometimes been followed with great success, but it can be extremely dangerous. Teaching the violin is really a job for the specialist, but if none is available this experiment is worth trying.

Few violin teachers have had an opportunity of being trained in the art of class teaching. Most of us have learned to play our instruments without ever dreaming that we ourselves would teach. When the time has come for us to take classes we are apt either to teach as we were taught, or to attempt to teach classes by instinct. We experiment on the poor wretches we teach, sometimes with success and sometimes with disastrous results.

Experiment can be most interesting and exciting, but it can also be wasteful. There are signs that some kind of help or training may be available in the future for string teachers as for teachers of other subjects, and this will save time and effort.

We need specialists for this work and it is encouraging to find that many violinists are becoming interested. Class teaching calls not only for teachers of sound musicianship with a knowledge of the basic skills, but for players. After hours of teaching this calls for tremendous effort, but I think it is important.

Above all, however, the teacher must feel enthusiasm for class teaching. To succeed it is essential to be genuinely interested in people as well as in music, and if the idea does not appeal it is better left alone. But any teacher attracted by this approach, and alive to the challenge it presents, will find it well worth carrying out, for it can give great satisfaction.

A question often asked is: 'For what purpose are you training children to play the violin when you teach them in class? As professionals or amateurs?' I understand what is implied by this question but the implication seems to me to be wrong.

It is always exciting to find exceptional talent; to discover that one has a pupil with great musical and manipulative ability, power of concentration and the capacity to work with intense application and even urgency. I have had the great good fortune to meet two such children out of many hundreds, and there has been little doubt from the beginning that these two would become professional violinists. But you can never be sure of any of the others and I have always tried to dissuade pupils from entering the musical profession if there is anything else in which they are remotely interested. It is unfortunate that when a child has some talent for the violin it is often assumed by parents or school that they will become professionals: this assumption and weight of opinion from outside can be very dangerous; and this is one of my main reasons for trying to persuade pupils to consider some other work. If they really want to become professional musicians, they will do so in spite of every discouragement. It will then be their choice and after that naturally one gives every possible assistance.

Another danger is that music 'happens' to people; they are not taught it and often do not choose it as a career. Thus it is vitally important to provide the right background and to help young people to use their tools properly from the very beginning.

There is no difference whatsoever in the early stages between a professional and an amateur. The teacher should regard every beginner, whether in class or not, as a potential Paganini. No one can tell what the outcome will be and it is not always the most talented who make the grade. Whether pupils become professionals or amateurs is irrelevant; all have potential ability and this means that the first lessons should be of the best and highest quality obtainable. Never should it be thought that second-rate lessons are good enough for beginners. The first five lessons are the ones that matter.

Important beyond everything is that the teachers should believe that every beginner is a potential virtuoso, that every child that comes for a first lesson will be a great musician and a brilliant violinist.

APPENDIX A

SOME CLASS TEACHING SCHEMES

A. *Primary School*

The instrumental teacher is a full-time member of staff. Pupils are selected in their second year at school, and lessons are given officially once a week in lunch hour. The teacher supervises practising in break, lunch hour and after school. There is no practice at home.

The school owns twelve instruments and each is used by several children. Some who are keen buy their own violins.

B. *Primary School*

The children are volunteers and are taught by a visiting teacher in small groups. There is close contact with the parents, some of whom are able to come to lessons to find out what work is being done and how it should be practised. Teaching takes place out of school hours. Children buy their instruments.

C. *Grammar School*

Every child entering the school learns a stringed instrument for one year. The lesson is one of two class music lessons in the week and is compulsory.

The school owns a very large number of instruments and can provide every child with a violin, viola, cello or bass. Classes average 45–50 children.

The music master is very experienced. He plans and gives the lesson, but calls on the visiting violin and cello teachers to help. He teaches from the back of the room at the piano, and the string specialists hover round their pupils keeping an eye on posture, bowing, wrists, etc.

An enormous amount of preparation is done on blackboards, each player reading in the appropriate clef for his instrument, and all playing together.

At the end of this year, pupils are taught in small groups or have private lessons out of school hours. Only one teacher in a hundred could work this plan.

D. *Grammar School*

Every child entering the school is given the choice of learning to play a violin or recorder for one term. Lessons are given in music class time, one of two music classes each week, by a visiting violin teacher.

The school owns fifteen violins, so fifteen pupils can be taught from each class. There are usually five or six classes.

This first term is a trial term and no practising is expected, but it is made clear to the children that if they wish to continue, practice will be essential, and they must then have their own instruments. There are various schemes for providing for easy purchase.

Those who find the violin is unsuited to them may leave off learning at the end of the term. Those who continue have two years in class. After that they take private lessons if they wish.

Viola and cello are taught out of school hours. The classes are usually small. In the second year, wind instrument classes begin.

E. *Secondary Modern School*

Ten pupils are very carefully selected from the A stream of children entering the school. Ear tests and manipulation tests are made, and ability to work and the home background are taken into account.

Lessons have been given at odd moments, during break, lunch hour or for a few minutes after school, by the teacher who is a member of the school staff.

There has been no wastage at all.

At the beginning of the second year these pupils become teachers to ten new beginners, and are responsible for their progress. Some of the first year group change over to viola, cello, flute and clarinet, but all start on the violin.

School instruments can be had on loan, but pupils are encouraged to buy their own as soon as possible.

F. Secondary Modern School

Every child entering the school has one music lesson a week. The school owns twenty violins, a number of descant recorders and percussion instruments. Violins and bows hang ready in glass fronted cupboards in the music room, recorders lie on trays, having been dipped in disinfectant at the end of every lesson, and percussion instruments are ready to hand on ledges and window sills.

During the first year, the music master plans his lessons so that all these instruments can be played together and combined with singing. A third of the class plays violins one week, recorders the next and then moves on to percussion for the third week and so back to the violins again, each type of instrument being used in rotation by every pupil. All music is arranged by the music master for every lesson and based on songs. At the end of the year he knows something of the potential ability of each pupil, and can arrange group lessons out of school hours. He himself teaches woodwind and brass and there are visiting violin and cello teachers. Instruments are always available during break and lunch hour and are practised in any available cloakroom or passage.

APPENDIX B

MUSIC LISTS

Published music used by one violin teacher with success may not necessarily suit another. The choice of material is a matter of personal taste and personal methods of teaching. A list made by one teacher would therefore help only a few. Instead, I suggest that all string teachers should make use of the following lists compiled by:

> The Rural Music Schools Association,
> > Little Benslow Hills,
> > > Hitchin, Herts.

1. Graded Music for String Class Teaching.
   (Violin, viola, cello, and bass)
2. A list of Chamber Music
   (Strings, strings and piano)
3. A Graded List of Orchestral Music.

These lists consist of music tried and recommended by experienced teachers and accepted by members of the advisory staff of the Rural Music Schools Association. Herein lies their value: for every work listed has been used with success by many teachers, each with an individual approach to the work, and although the lists are not exhaustive they are comprehensive enough to cover a wide variety of teaching methods. As new works are published and tried out in instrumental classes, so reports will be received by the Association and supplementary lists will be issued.

APPENDIX C

CARE AND REPAIR OF THE VIOLIN

It is the responsibility of the teacher to see that instruments are maintained in good working order.

Every beginner should have a clean, well-fitted violin and bow for the first lesson, and whenever possible the initial overhaul of the instrument should be done by a skilled craftsman. It is not always easy to find an expert, and sometimes the instruments are of such inferior quality that one hesitates to ask an experienced violin repairer to use his skill and spend his time working on poor material.

Some teachers are themselves expert craftsmen. Not only can they deal with external fittings, but they can set a sound post, repair a bow, or glue cracks. Not every teacher has the interest or ability to do this work, but if all could do the following repairs much valuable time would be saved.

1. Clean the instrument (special liquid cleaner can be obtained for this purpose).
2. Replace a broken tail-piece gut.
3. Replace a broken bridge.
4. Ease pegs (special peg paste can be obtained, but flour or dry soap may be used).
5. Oil bow-screws.
6. Wash the hair of the bow.
7. String the violin correctly.
8. Fit a chin-rest and steel string adjuster.

It is best to learn these skills from someone already experienced in this work. For those unable to obtain this practical help there is a booklet that may be useful:

Champ, Stephen.   *The Violin Pupil and the care of the Instrument*. Strad.

The concise instructions and clear illustrations are helpful to the amateur craftsman.

APPENDIX D

CHARTS

It is possible to buy large cards, special ink and felt pens for the making of charts, but they can also be made quickly on white kitchen paper. They are much lighter to carry than those made on stronger paper or card, and if they tear they can be renewed easily and at little cost.

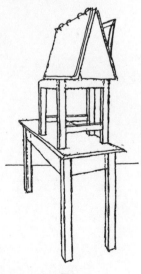

Fig. 46

It is best to place these charts between hardboard covers, held together as in a loose-leaf notebook by hinged rings or spring key rings. The cover not only protects the paper but makes it possible for the charts to be displayed flat on a blackboard or easel, or with the free sides of the hardboard a few inches apart the charts will stand without support on the top of the piano or on a chair standing on a desk (see fig. 46). There is then no need to pin up charts with drawing pins or spend much time before the lessons writing tunes on the blackboard.

The size of chart most satisfactory for a class of eight or ten pupils is 30 inches by 20 inches.

Three staves can be drawn clearly on each chart, the width of the stave being about 3 inches and the distance between each stave is also 3 inches. The lines of the stave, clef, time signatures, key signatures and stems of notes may be drawn with thick black crayon and the note heads painted in black ink with a brush.

APPENDIX E

STRINGS

There is considerable difference of opinion as to the most suitable type of strings for violin class pupils. The most usual set is:

E   Steel (wire) with adjuster
A   Gut
D   Gut
G   Covered gut

The alternative is all-steel strings. The initial cost of steel strings (with the necessary adjusters or special tailpiece with built-in adjusters) is greater than that of gut, but it has been found that the problem of tuning is eased by the use of steel strings even if the tone quality (particularly in the early stages of pizzicato) is not so pleasant.

If steel strings are used, every string *must* have an adjuster and a lower bridge must be fitted. The strange combination of gut strings attached to adjusters or steel strings without this attachment should be avoided at all cost. The teacher would be wise to keep a stock of strings for sale, he can then be certain that pupils are provided with the right kind.

APPENDIX F

BOOK LIST

Aulich and Heimeran. *The Well-Tempered String Quartet*. Novello.

Brown, Hullah. *Instrumental Music in Schools*. Pitman.

Carse, Adam. *The School Orchestra*. Williams.

Champ, Stephen. *The Violin Pupil and the Care of the Instrument*. Strad.

Farga, Franz. *Violins and Violinists*. Rockliff.

Flesch, Carl. *Problems of tone production in Violin Playing*. Fischer.

Jacob, Gordon. *How to read a score*. Boosey and Hawkes.

Jacobsen, Maxim. *The Mastery of Violin Playing*. Boosey and Hawkes.

Kinsey, Herbert. *The Foundations of Violin Playing and Musicianship*. Longman.

Knocker, Editha. *The Violin* (Festival Booklet). Peterson.

Knocker, Editha. *The Violinist's Vade Mecum*. Curwen.

Leland, Valborg. *The Dounis Principles of Violin Playing*. Strad.

Mangeot, André. *Violin Technique*. Dobson.

Robjohns, Sydney. *Violin Technique*. O.U.P.

Scott, M. M. *What can I play?* Quality Press.

Slater, Moira. *Bows and Strings*. Knox, Durban.

Stratton and Frank. *Chamber Music*. Dobson.

Wessley, H. *A Practical Guide to Violin Playing*. Williams.

The Scope of Instrumental Music in Schools. National Council of Social Service, London.

PRINTED IN GREAT BRITAIN
BY EBENEZER BAYLIS AND SON, LTD.
THE TRINITY PRESS
WORCESTER AND LONDON